The
Other Side of
Love

The Other Side of Love

Story by Attilio Guardo

ReadersMagnet, LLC

Conrad Arlington Hill sat slumped in a chair on the gazebo, his face a reflection of despondency. For the past two months his being had wallowed in the abysmal pits of depression, in sharp contrast to the ecstatic heights of love it had known a few months ago. Oh, how beautiful life had been.

The gazebo and the surrounding beautifully landscaped grounds had become one of his favorite places, and when he had shared it with his love Abigail McCloud, he had looked upon it as a small piece of paradise. The grounds had not changed, but to him the beauty was now gone. Abigail McCloud suddenly had decided she no longer wanted to be a part of his life. He had trusted her with his heart and she had totally destroyed it, and it was as though the life force had been sucked from his body.

Since that time he virtually had done nothing but exist. He had experienced trouble sleeping, his appetite had become irregular, and he had lost the ability to concentrate for any length of time. Fortunately, he had been able to take a leave of absence from his father's business. In essence, everything had lost its purpose and meaning, and his life had become one of deliberate seclusion. Even his exposure to his parents and the two family servants had become minimal.

After one month, Conrad's pain had slightly abated, but his hatred for Abigail had intensified. He had tried to put her out of his mind, but his efforts had been futile. At first, he wrestled with the idea of again pleading with her to marry him and give him a chance to give her the world. He had then convinced himself however, that perhaps she really didn't care about him anymore. And no, he wouldn't plead with her to come back anymore, for he did still manage to have some pride. He wouldn't let the miserable bitch destroy that too.

Conrad got up from the chair and slowly walked over to the railing of the gazebo and leaned on it with his arms. A lone, long stemmed flower extended through the pickets and brushed his leg. "A lonely flower and a lonely man," he whispered despondently, and he reached down and severed the stem. He raised the flower to his eyes, and for a moment stared at it as if immersed in some past recollection. He held it in his hand, and as he walked back to the chair he felt a sense of solace. Slowly sitting down, he stared into the distance unaware of the flower gracefully twirling in his fingers. He still did not understand how Abigail could have changed her emotions so suddenly and so insensitively ended their relationship. And he probably never would.

Conrad rested his head against the back of the chair and his thoughts drifted back to Abigail. He was convinced she had loved him. She had to. She never would have said and done the things she did. He thought about the times she would call him when they were not able to see each other.

"I love you, Conrad, more than ever," she would say. The words would always nourish his soul, and it would always solidify his love for her.

"I love you too, more than ever. And I miss you," he would answer.

"Miss you too, Conrad. I wish we were together now."

"We will be tomorrow. Take care of yourself and think of me."

"Of course I will, my love. I think of you all the time."

He thought of the times he said, "I am going to marry you, Abigail." She would answer, "You better. I want to spend the rest of my life with you."

"Don't worry, my love. We will be together until the end of time," he would reassure her.

Conrad was reliving it all over again and he couldn't stop himself. It was like a self-inflicted pain that cut deeper and deeper into his heart. Oh, how he had loved her. He would have truly placed her on a pedestal and given her the world. She would have been his princess, his queen, and his existence.

How well he remembered calling her his queen and she saying, "I am your queen only if you're my king."

"What a beautiful thing to say," he would tell her, and she would look at him with loving eyes, smiling softly and raising his spirits to the heights of heaven.

"Don't ever leave me, Abigail," he would say.

"Never, my love," she would reply. I would rather die first than give you up," she would assure him. But she had given him up. And when he had asked her why, all she had said was she no longer could handle their relationship.

He thought of all the words of commitment she had spoken to him over the past year. He had believed her with all his heart, and when she reneged on them he had found it totally incomprehensible.

Conrad rose from the chair, his breath quickening in anger. "The phony, lying bitch," he said in despair. "How could she do this to me," and he paced back and forth like a restless beast in a cage. "I was good to her, so good to her. I could have made her happy. The stupid bitch never gave me a chance," and he was again conversing with himself aloud. His anger and hatred were intensifying. He wondered why she had come into his life, and he wished he had never met her.

Contrary to how he wanted to feel, a part of him still loved her, and deep in his heart he still wanted her. He wasn't able to remove her from his memory, and it kindled his self-wrath. Whenever he found himself thinking how beautiful it was between them, it angered him all the more, and the venom of hate pumped harder through his body.

"I do hate the phony, miserable bitch," he told himself over and over again. A part of him did hate her, but it wasn't enough. His whole being had to hate her if he was going to live without her. He was engaged in an emotional war with himself; a war he had to win for his survival.

That night Conrad lay awake in his bed. To sleep was hopeless. When Abigail had first left him, he had contemplated suicide but then had dismissed the idea. Now he had to think of a way to get even. By nature, he wasn't a hateful, vindictive man. But now that did not matter. There must be no more love for Abigail.

By morning he had worked up a renewed, profound hatred. "The no good, phony bitch will pay," he vowed aloud to himself. She was a woman who had sinned against him, and he could never condone her. Because of her, he now looked upon all women as evil, and he vowed he would never love again. He would make them pay for his hurt, and it didn't matter who they were. No one would ever be worthy of him again, and he decided it was time to start on his mission of vengeance.

CHAPTER 2

It was nine in the morning when Conrad was awakened by the buzzing of his intercom.

"Mr. Conrad, wake up," said the voice over the intercom. "You have a phone call. Please pick up."

Conrad glanced at the clock next to his bed, and he could not believe he had slept so late. It marked the first time in over a month he had not been awake before six in the morning.

"Mr. Conrad, please pick up," the voice repeated.

Conrad depressed the button on the intercom. "Who is it?" he asked.

"A Mr. Ed McDowell is on the phone. He said he is an ex-army friend of yours."

Of course, Ed McDowell, thought Conrad. He had not heard from him in four years, and now he was suddenly on the phone.

"Thank you, Sadie," said Conrad, and he picked up the receiver. "For Christ sake, if it isn't Ed McDowell. How the hell are you?"

"I'm okay, Conrad. How are you doing, buddy?"

"I'm hanging in there these days, Ed."

"Well, I hope it's not by the neck," Ed said jokingly.

"Considering the past couple months, sometimes I wonder," said Conrad with a serious voice.

Ed hesitated. "Sounds serious, Is it?"

Conrad let out a sigh. "When I feel like talking and you feel like listening, I might tell you."

"Tell me, Ed, where are you calling from?"

"I'm at the Holiday Inn in downtown Fairfield."

"Great, you're in town. What brings you to Connecticut?"

Ed cleared his throat. "Since I am unemployed at the moment, I thought I would get away from Pennsylvania for a while. Work wise things have not been going to well for me, and I decided it might be a good idea to talk to some of the acting agencies in New York," and Ed forced himself to sound optimistic.

"I see. Are you driving?" asked Conrad.

"Yes, buddy. I drove in from Pennsylvania last night."

"Tell you what, Ed. You are only ten minutes from the house. Why don't you drive over and we can talk about old times."

"Sounds good, buddy," said Ed.

"Let me give you some directions. The place is easy to find. Stay on I-95 east, take exit 22 and hang a right. That's route 4, and stay on it until you come to Manor Acres. We are the second house on the right about a mile from the entrance."

"I have it, Conrad. I'll see you in a little while."

"Ed, I'm glad you called. I am looking forward to seeing you," and there was sincerity in Conrad's voice.

Yes, he was looking forward to Ed's visit even though it was unexpected and sudden. He had been out of circulation for the past two months and he desperately needed a change. He could trust Ed. They had been the best of friends during their three-year military hitch, and they had had some great times together.

Conrad quickly showered and had some juice and toast and was ready for Ed's arrival.

When Ed drove through the open gateway and along the entrance that brought him to the Hill mini mansion, he was overwhelmed. He knew Conrad came from a family of good financial means based on what little information Conrad had volunteered in the past, but what he saw was entirely different from what he had imagined.

The structure was an elegant turn of the century Victorian, which housed sixteen rooms and was three levels high. Six chimneys emerged from the roof. Three quarters of the structure was surrounded by an open porch which ran continuously from the main entrance along both sides. The house sat on fifteen acres of fields and woodlands. The area around the house was tastefully landscaped with a variety of contrasting shrubs and flowers, and it was evident the grounds were meticulously maintained. A large, Italian fountain was stationed adjacent to the front entrance. A renovated carriage house, which housed the four family cars, stood forty yards behind the main structure.

"This is some place," Ed said softly, and the atmosphere associated with it was something he definitely was not accustomed to.

As Ed was getting out of the car, Conrad was on his way to greet him. "Conrad, how nice to see you," said Ed, and he gave him a manly hug.

"It's great seeing you again, Ed. Come on in and meet my mother."

"This is some place you people have here. It's simply beautiful," said Ed as they walked into the foyer. Ed's eyes quickly scanned the foyer, the adjoining sitting room and the massive mahogany staircase that led to the second floor, and he could not conceal his feeling of amazement.

"Just beautiful," said Ed almost involuntarily. "This place blows my mind."

"You get use to it after a while. It's just like anything else," said Conrad with an attitude of indifference. He had been exposed to wealth and the comforts of life associated with it at a very early age. He never had to think about anything else. His only deviation from upper class living had come when he volunteered for military service at the age of eighteen. He had made the decision against the judgment of his family who insisted he foolishly wasted three valuable years of his life. To Conrad it was independence and rebellion from the dominance of his parents who were always much too eager to decide the direction his life should go.

Conrad had just brought Ed into the sitting room when Sadie, one of the servants, entered the room.

"Sadie," said Conrad, this is Ed McDowell, an ex-army friend. Would you please tell mother I would like her to meet him?"

"Yes, Mr. Conrad. I will give her the message immediately," and Sadie walked briskly out of the room.

"Get comfortable on a chair, Ed," Conrad offered.

Ed seated himself on a late, 19th century Victorian sofa.

"I don't know how comfortable you will find that sofa," commented Conrad. This damn furniture is pretty to look at but leaves a lot to be desired for comfort. My mother is a formal decorating enthusiast, and there is no chance of changing that. As for me, I'll take the conventional, more comfortable stuff."

"The chairs fine, Conrad," said Ed evenly.

"Can I get you a drink?" Conrad offered.

"No, thanks, buddy. Maybe I'll have one a little later."

Conrad seated himself opposite Ed. "So tell me, what has been happening in your life, Ed? Last time I saw you, you took on a new bride. How is Shelly?"

"Well," Ed paused. "Shelly and I split up last year. Things just didn't work out for us."

"I'm sorry to hear that, Ed," and Conrad was truly sorry. He thought about his own loss of Abigail. Conrad was about to speak when his mother appeared at the entrance of the room.

Constance Hill was an elegant woman in her early fifties with dark hair that was streaked with gray at the sides. She was of medium height and build, and had the posture of a soldier. As she entered the room, both men rose from their seats.

"Mother, this is Ed McDowell, and old army friend. Ed, this is my mother Constance."

"Pleased to meet you, Ed," and Constance offered her hand.

"Pleased meeting you, Mrs. Hill. You really have a beautiful home here."

"I think so, thank you. My husband has worked very hard for what he has attained," she replied with sharpness in her voice. "I do not know what your plans are, but I want you to know you are welcome to stay with us if you like."

"Thank you, Mrs. Hill. I appreciate your most generous offer."

"Well, I am sure you gentlemen have a great deal to talk about, and I have a club luncheon to attend." Constance started to leave the room and then stopped and turned. Then she said, "Conrad, why don't you show our home to Ed? This way he will have an idea where things are in the event he decides to stay."

"Yes, mother, I will."

"Thank you again, Mrs. Hill. You are most gracious," and Ed smiled appreciatively.

The two men seated themselves. "Your mother is one proud woman," said Ed.

"Oh yes," agreed Conrad, "Proud and very confident. Let's see now, Ed, you were telling me that you and Shelly had split up when mother entered the room."

"That's correct," said Ed, and he shifted his body on the sofa. "I guess we never had a good marriage from the beginning. Shelly needed financial security, and I guess I could never give it to her. She is the type who needs someone with a solid position in a company who definitely is going up the ladder. She didn't appreciate my trying to pursue an acting career. When I had acting jobs it wasn't too bad. But when there was no work I had to take what I could find, and often the jobs didn't pay very well. That is when the arguments would start," and Ed shook his head remorsefully. "I guess," Ed continued, "she thought I was wasting my time in the amateur circuit, and in a field so competitive that few people make it to the top. Perhaps she was right. I have gone nowhere. I guess I should have known better."

"Shit, Ed," Conrad interjected. "Life is full of uncertainties. It goes from good to bad, bad to good. In my opinion, life is like a damn predator and we people are its prey. We have to look out for our asses, but sooner or later we all fall victims to it. It grabbed me by the balls two months ago and I am still feeling the pain. You have to fight back and get even. Yes, that is what you have to do," said Conrad, and he clenched his hand into a fist. "I need a damn drink," he said suddenly. "And would you like a drink, Ed?" Conrad asked.

"Okay, you talked me into it. I will have a beer."

"Good. Hang tight, and I will be right back," and Ed watched him leave the room.

Ed was observant enough to notice during the brief time of his visit that Conrad wasn't the same easy going, carefree person he had known four years ago. He was seeing a different man who apparently was down on life. Why? Ed wondered. He has so much going for him. He was good looking, educated, intelligent and had the resources to buy anything he desired. Here was a man who possessed the enviable combination of personal qualities and economic status that most women would find irresistible, and Ed wished he himself could be so fortunate.

He thought about the conversation he had had with Conrad earlier in the day and the comments Conrad had made about hanging in there these days. Ed knew Conrad well enough to know that he disliked being probed for information, and if there was something he wanted to say he would say it when he was ready. He would wait for Conrad to initiate any conversation relevant to his personal life.

"Ed," said Conrad as he returned with the drinks. "Why don't we sit and relax outside by the pool?"

"Sure, buddy. It sounds great."

Conrad led Ed into the library where there were two French doors that opened onto a patio of red, roman bricks that surrounded a large, kidney shaped swimming pool. Tastefully scattered around the outer perimeter of the patio were a half dozen brick planters containing shrubs and flowers.

"What a spot," said Ed, and he again found himself commenting on yet another beautiful sight. "I could get use to this place in a second."

Conrad looked at Ed and smiled. "Abigail loved it too," and then the smile left his face.

The two men seated themselves, and for a moment Conrad stared at the water and seemed distant.

"You know Ed, I can relate to your experience with Shelly. I was going with a girl for about a year when she suddenly decided she didn't want me anymore. I thought she was going to be my whole life."

"I assume the girl is Abigail," said Ed.

"Yes, Abigail Theresa McCloud," said Conrad, and he paused to sip his drink. "The bitch has destroyed me Ed," Conrad said painfully. "The last two months have been hell. I have not worked and I have not had a decent nights sleep until last night. I have tried to forget her, but I can't."

So that was it, thought Ed. Conrad had fallen in love and had been dumped, and apparently hard. He knew it couldn't have been just a matter of ego even though Conrad was in the habit of getting what he wanted. It had to go beyond that. He remembered Conrad saying in the past that when he fell in love it would be for life, and he had fallen in love, the poor bastard.

"I'm sorry it happened to you, buddy," Ed said sympathetically. "I wish there was something I could do."

Conrad studied Ed for a moment and then said, "Maybe there is something you can do for me."

"Sure, buddy. Just name it."

Conrad had been thinking. When Ed had mentioned his acting endeavors, an idea had entered his mind. He remembered how well Ed had acted in a couple of stage productions sponsored by the military for the entertainment of their personnel. He was good. Now he would have the opportunity to act in his greatest role, and Conrad would be the director.

"I have an idea, Ed, but for it to work I need your help. First, I know you are not working and I know why you drove in from Pennsylvania. That tends to make things a little less complicated. I will get right to the point. I have an acting role for you. There will be one other character involved. The two of you will play yourselves.

Even the plot will be real. I think you will find it most interesting, Ed," Conrad said confidently.

Ed looked at Conrad quizzically. "I don't understand how my acting in a role will help you, buddy. And who is this other character?"

Conrad gave Ed a long stare and said, "Abigail McCloud."

Ed was suddenly puzzled. Conrad had not given him all the details and Ed's curiosity was totally aroused. "I don't understand," he said.

"Very simply my friend, you will date Abigail and make her fall in love with you. When she does and she is most vulnerable, you will drop the bitch and let her feel the pain."

Ed could see Conrad's eyes had become full of hate and it made him apprehensive. "But what… what if she doesn't care for me?" Ed asked awkwardly.

"She loves the theatre, and you are an actor in search of bigger and better things. Besides, you are a good-looking guy and you know how to charm women. I know you will be able to do this," Conrad assured him. "Just give it your best shot and we'll see what happens."

Ed stirred uneasily in his chair and in his heart he was hoping Conrad would call the whole thing off. But he didn't.

"I have it all figured out, Ed," continued Conrad. "I will give you all the directions you need to pull this off; and we won't rest until the mission has been executed," and he downed the remainder of his drink. "Trust me, we are friends, remember?"

The whole conversation had caught Ed by surprise, and to make matters worse, he had already committed himself to helping Conrad before he had heard the details. The whole idea of him assisting Conrad to get even with Abigail was starting to make him very uncomfortable.

"Well, what do you say? Will you do it?" asked Conrad.

Ed honestly didn't like it, but he did owe Conrad for several past favors. He wondered what he would be getting into. Reluctantly, he would do it. "Sure, buddy," he agreed.

"Great," said Conrad, and he was pleased. "Now let me do some explaining," and he moved forward to the end of his chair. "You will need a place to stay. No problem. My father owns some condos about ten minutes from here and there are some vacancies. I will set you up there. Now let us look at the financial implications. I will cover all the necessary costs you incur in carrying out your mission."

Your mission, thought Ed. It was a throw back to their military days where one's assignment was called a mission, and Conrad was now detailing him like a sergeant.

Conrad sat back in his chair for a moment scratching his chin as if he was pondering what he was going to say next. "Since we do not know exactly how long this will take, I am going to pay you a weekly salary of three hundred dollars. I want the bitch badly, Ed, but at the same time I do not want to be unreasonable where you are concerned and cause you any hardships. Hopefully, what we are doing will not change your life style or your endeavors to pursue your career. Actually, I feel Abigail will be more impressed if you are working and she can see you performing locally or in New York. But, if you do not find work look at it this way, in the interim you have an acting job and I am the producer-director. Together we will make our production a success. "Fair enough?" asked Conrad.

"Fair enough," answered Ed, and Conrad's concern for his personal life was of some consolation to him. But he still remained skeptical about the plan working. It really depended entirely on Abigail and how receptive she would be when he tried to make her acquaintance. All he could do was try his best. Two more questions had to be answered.

"When and how do you want me to start, Conrad?" Ed asked.

"I want to start tomorrow," said Conrad with a vindictive grin. "As to how, I have not quite decided. There are a few details I want to sort out in my mind. I will let you know in the morning."

So I will know in the morning, thought Ed. He again hoped it would work. If it did not, he was sure Conrad would take another course of action, and he did not want to speculate on what that might be. From what he had seen he was sure of one thing, Conrad would not back down.

That night Conrad lay awake in bed and thought how strange it was that Ed should suddenly call him, and that he was an actor who was out of work. It was all so appropriate and the timing was perfect. It had to be more than mere coincidence. It was an act of fate that was assisting him. Yes, that is what it had to be. To Conrad, it was an omen the gods of vengeance were on his side, and he fell asleep smiling.

CHAPTER 3

Conrad had insisted Ed stay overnight. The events of the day and the anticipation of the role he was about to play had weighed on Ed's mind, and as a result he had had a restless night.

Immediately following an early breakfast, Conrad took Ed to see the condominiums at High Point and gave him a tour of the facilities. Later, Conrad took the liberty of selecting Ed a comfortable unit which consisted of two bedrooms, a living room with a stone fireplace, a dining room and a bright kitchen. There was a balcony off the living room that overlooked a small, man-made pond where two white swans floated gracefully on the placid water. A small, wooden bridge arched over a portion of the pond where the water jutted into the land.

Conrad thought his choice of the living quarters was perfect for an aspiring actor. "You should be more than comfortable here, Ed," said Conrad authoritatively. "I think the view from here is great."

"No question about it. The place is beautiful," said Ed, and he was truly delighted. "I love the wooded surroundings and the privacy," and he walked out onto the balcony.

"Don't worry about furnishing the place," Conrad was saying, and Ed wasn't listening to him. He was thinking of Shelly. To him, there was no doubt she would have loved such a place. She would have marveled at the layout, the serenity and the non-debatable class of High Point. He couldn't help speculate that things would have been different between them if they could have shared such a lavish home and he had had a secure position in a company. He found himself almost wishing she were with him now, sharing the view, for he was still admittedly in love with her.

Conrad walked up to Ed and placed his hand on his shoulder. "Ed, you don't have to worry about furnishing this place," he repeated.

"I'm sorry, buddy," Ed apologized. "I guess I kind of drifted away."

"I will have this place furnished by the end of the day," promised Conrad. "There is some furniture available here that the management uses to furnish the model units. I will instruct the superintendent to see to it that your unit is properly furnished by the end of the day. If it isn't, I'll fire his ass."

Conrad's remark made Ed think how nice it was to have power. Conrad appeared to have everything under control at this point, and he had Ed beginning to believe that the remainder of his planning would be impeccable.

"This is what our itinerary will be for the remainder of the day," continued Conrad. "I will take you back to the house so that you can pick up your car. Then take the afternoon to buy whatever clothing and supplies you will need for the time being so that you can move into the condo today," and Conrad handed him a role of money.

Ed felt uncomfortable taking it, but then reconciled to the fact the whole scheme was Conrad's idea and that he was merely helping him out. After all, he had been hired to do a job, hadn't he?

"Sure, buddy," agreed Ed.

"I have a few matters myself that I have to attend to," said Conrad. I'll meet you back here at six this evening. It should be mutually convenient. We can have an early dinner at the Ivanhoe House. I'll reserve a private corner, and while we are eating I'll go over my plan as to how you will meet Abigail."

"Sounds good, buddy," and though Ed didn't show it, he was most anxious to know what Conrad had planned. His aroused curiosity was turning into anxiety and Conrad wasn't making it any easier for him. True, he was an actor, but he was being assigned a unique role. He would be playing with his own emotions and the true emotions of a girl he didn't even know. If she did fall in love with him he would be playing with her heart, manipulating it deliberately so he could deal it a crushing blow.

Conrad left and Ed went about buying the essentials he needed. Much to his own surprise he found himself wondering for most of the afternoon what Abigail was like. He even went so far as to envision her physical attributes. He was naturally curious and at the same time a sense of compassion for his pending victim started to creep into him. Ed was intelligent enough to know he couldn't let that happen. He had to maintain his personal sense of apathy, no matter what.

When Ed arrived at the condo, Conrad was already there. "Your condo is in order, Ed. I guess I don't get to fire the superintendent's ass," commented Conrad with a grin.

Ed was pleased with the furnishings. "Thanks buddy," he said appreciatively.

"How did your afternoon go?" asked Conrad.

"Good, real good," said Ed.

"Why don't I give you a hand unloading your car?"

"Great, buddy. I accept your offer. And thanks"

Later, when they had unloaded Ed's car they went to the Ivanhoe House for dinner. Ed found the restaurant to be every bit what he had anticipated, plush, expensive and rich with atmosphere. When the maitre d saw Conrad, he immediately came over. "Good Evening, Mr. Hill, your table is ready," and he led them to a private table. "I'll send your waiter over immediately, and have a pleasant evening, gentlemen."

"You will find the food is excellent and the service just as good," vouched Conrad.

"I don't find it surprising," said Ed.

"The house specialty is Beef Wellington. You really should try it."

"It sounds good to me, buddy."

When the entrée was placed before him, Ed was astounded at the size and artistic display before him. He stared at the plate for a moment before he commented, "Am I suppose to eat this? I fell like a barbarian destroying such a beautiful piece of art."

"Go for it, Ed," and Conrad smiled.

"Well, Ed, you must be wondering how I intend to start matters rolling. Like my father, I prefer to discuss business over a good meal. Great Guy, my father," and Ed wasn't quite sure if Conrad's remark was intended to denote sincerity or sarcasm. Anyway, he wished Conrad would refrain with the small talk and get to the point. How was he going to meet Abigail?

"I thought I would try a more conventional approach," said Conrad as he raised a glass of red wine to his lips. "Every Saturday morning Abigail does volunteer work at the Fairfield County Hospital. She has a habit of being remarkably punctual. I can assure you she will be leaving at twelve noon sharp. When she does she will discover, and much to her dismay, that she has a flat tire," and Conrad grinned slyly.

"I see," Ed said softly. "I am assuming I some how come to her rescue."

"You have it right my friend. Let me clue you in on the mechanics of my plan. First, we will take two cars to the hospital and I will identify her car. Then in an inconspicuous manner you will remove the air from one of her tires." He paused to drink more wine and pour another glass. He rattled on. "You will offer to change her tire; by changing her tire you will look like a macho hero and a gentleman. How does it sound?" Conrad asked.

"Sounds good," agreed Ed thinking it was a good approach.

"I will see to it that I leave in plenty of time before Abigail makes her grand entrance onto the stage. I don't want to risk blowing it before it gets started." Conrad hesitated and then spoke. "Shit, I almost forgot to mention the timing aspect of your initial contact. You will park your car, circumstances permitting, relatively close to hers. I will see to it tomorrow morning that you have a picture of her so you will know what she looks like. When you see her approaching her car, that's the time you should leave your car and start walking towards her." Conrad stared at Ed and smiled.

"I leave the rest in your hands. I'll be expecting to hear from you sometime tomorrow telling me it went well and that you are on the way to devouring your prey." Conrad paused and leaned forward in his chair. "Ed, if you fail, I'll hang your balls in effigy," he said softly, and Ed wondered just how much humor was in Conrad's remark.

Conrad took his glass in his hand and said, "Why don't we call it a night. But first a toast to the success of our production which will commence tomorrow," and they raised their glasses.

It was an over-cast Saturday morning and the air was heavy with humidity. Ed's mind was equally heavy with concern. He had to make Conrad's plan work so he could see Abigail again. If it didn't, it would be almost impossible to get a second chance without arousing her suspicion. He felt like a quarterback with one play left to try and score before time ran out. Most of all he didn't want to fail Conrad.

Conrad arrived at the condo at eleven in the morning. He refreshed Ed's memory on the mechanics of the plan. Then he handed him a picture of Abigail. Everything was ready for the production to roll.

Ed followed Conrad down to the hospital parking lot. When they entered the lot Conrad drove through slowly as he searched for Abigail's car, and Ed wondered if it was there. Suddenly, Conrad stopped and got out of his car and walked over to Ed. "Her car is that white Cutlass. Luckily there is a vacant spot close by. Take it and I'll see you there in a few minutes."

Ed parked and in a moment Conrad was at his window. "This is it, Ed. I know you can do it. Good, luck," and Conrad reached in and shook his hand. "I'll be waiting for your call," and he walked away.

Ed looked in his rear view mirror and saw Conrad exiting the lot. It was a quarter to twelve. He didn't have much time. He got out of the car and started walking toward Abigail's Cutlass. His eyes were nervously scanning the area around her car to make certain no one would be in a position to observe him.

When he was next to it, he dropped down beside the left front tire and depressed the valve. The air hissed out and it seemed to take an eternity. When the tire was flat he stood up casually and looked around. He was relieved that no one was paying attention to him, and he slowly walked back to his car. It was almost noon. He waited, and he felt unusually nervous, and it annoyed him. It was not unusual for him to feel some nervousness before he went on stage. It was no different now, and he told himself he was being foolish. She was just another girl.

Then Ed saw her. He strained his eyes and then looked at the picture. It was Abigail and she was proceeding toward her car. He remembered Conrad saying the timing was important so he waited for her to get closer. "Now," he said, and he opened the door. He started walking toward her when he noticed a gentleman approaching her from another direction. He heard the man say, "Hi, Abigail," and he started to walk with her.

"Shit," grumbled Ed. "The son-of-a-bitch is going to ruin everything. He is going to offer to change her tire."

The unexpected had materialized, and now it had to be counter acted. He had to do something, and his mind started racing. He would convince them he could best remedy the problem. Ed walked faster and he arrived at the car a few seconds after Abigail and the gentleman.

"Do you have a spare?" the gentleman was asking.

"Thank, God, I do," she said emphatically.

"Good, I'll take care of it for you," and as he started for the trunk of the car it started to rain.

"Pardon me," Ed interrupted tactfully, and they both turned and faced him. "Can I offer some assistance?"

The gentleman looked at Ed indignantly. "That's okay, I'll handle it," he said, and a light rain continued to fall.

As the gentleman started for the trunk, his pager beeped. He immediately pulled it from his belt and glanced at it with a frown. "I'm sorry, Abigail," he said as he returned the pager to his belt. "I have to get back to the hospital for an emergency. I guess this gentleman will have to help you after all."

"Thank you, Carl. I'll talk to you later."

Abigail looked at Ed and smiled. "A flat tire, rain the first time in over a month, and Carl getting called on an emergency could have been a real disaster if you hadn't come along. If we were in England instead of New England I could dub thee Sir… What would I dub thee?"

"Ed, Ed McDowell. And you would be Queen…?"

"Abigail McCloud."

"Yes, I know," he said to himself as he gazed into her brown eyes. He had accomplished Phase I consisting of establishing contact. Now the more difficult Phase II, charming her and winning her confidence.

Ed walked back to the trunk and removed the spare tire and jack. He immediately began to remove the flat tire as the rain descended with more intensity.

Abigail reached into the back seat of the car and pulled out an umbrella. She opened it and placed it over Ed to shield him from the rain.

"Since I'm not able to assist you, at least I can keep you from drowning."

After changing the tire, Ed quickly returned the flat tire and jack to the trunk and said, "Your tire should be all set now, but don't forget to get the spare fixed. You never know when fate will strike again." And as his smile broadened, their eyes meet with an unexplainable presence of warmth, much like the early morning sun welcoming a new day. They stood there for a moment, looking into each other's eyes. It was Ed who spoke first. "According to the tag you are wearing, I see you do volunteer work."

She was wearing a hospital tag that read volunteer worker and he had observed it.

"Yes, I do, and it's something I really enjoy doing," she said.

"I know what you mean. I do some on occasion myself. I am an actor by profession and I do a clown sketch for the children."

"So, you are an actor. How fascinating," said Abigail, "You certainly are a pretty special person to give your time to sick children."

"Thanks, but it isn't all that special. You see, if I can help them forget their illness even for a short while, it gives me a feeling that my life is more meaningful. So I guess you could say it's a two way street."

"Now tell me, what part of the hospital is fortunate to have someone as lovely as you to look forward to?"

"I spend most of my time with the elderly," she said.

"I think that's great," he said commendably. "Sooner or later we all reach that point in life."

The rain tapped harder on the umbrella making them realize they had become oblivious to it.

"Here we are talking in the rain like a couple of ducks," Abigail said jokingly, and suddenly she knew she wanted to see him again. She was attracted to his friendly demeanor and physical appearance. He stood six feet tall, and gave the impression that he was athletic. He had straight, sandy brown hair and hazel colored eyes that were both friendly and captivating. His forehead was square and strong, and she loved his gracious smile and the patch of freckles that ran across his upper nose and extended to his cheeks. Yes, she liked him.

Sensing she found him attractive, Ed said, "I have a wonderful idea. Why don't we discuss our work over dinner tomorrow night?" I must warn you I won't take no for an answer."

She was flattered, and she loved it. She would love to go, but did not want to look too eager. She paused as if in thought and then answered, "It just happens I'm free tomorrow night. I accept."

"I am honored and delighted that you accept. I'll pick you up at seven in the evening. If you give me your phone number I'll call you for directions."

She could never know how delighted he was. He had pulled it off. Phase II of their plan was successful, and Conrad would be pleased.

Abigail got into the car and he closed the door behind her. "Drive carefully," he said.

"You too, and thanks again."

As he walked back to his car he watched her drive away.

The drive back to the condominium seemed to be shorter, perhaps because his mind had been preoccupied with Abigail the entire time. She seemed like a warm, tender person, and he wondered what had happened between her and Conrad.

The first thing Ed did upon entering the condo was to mix a scotch and soda. He toasted himself on a job well done and sat down on the couch. "Now to call the producer," he commanded himself, and he reached over and picked up the phone.

The phone rang only once before he heard Conrad say, "Hello."

"Conrad, this is Ed."

"Yes, Ed. How did it go?" he asked anxiously.

"We did it. I'm taking her to dinner tomorrow night."

"Son-of-a-bitch, I knew you could do it," and he was ecstatic. "Did it go like we planned?"

"It was smooth. She bought the tire completely. There was one unexpected incident, but I handled it."

"Ed, when this thing is over I'll see to it that you get an Emmy award, Solid Gold."

Ed laughed. "I appreciate your confidence in me buddy, but I have a hell of a lot more acting to do."

"You will do just fine. I'll call you tomorrow before your dinner engagement."

"Okay, Conrad. Take care, buddy."

Conrad felt good. The bitch had fallen for the initial introduction, and she would be falling for a great deal more. Yes, he felt good and he couldn't wait for the dramatic ending. He had planted the seeds of vengeance, and it now was up to Ed to cultivate and nourish them. Meanwhile, he was ready to set the stage for himself and do some acting of his own while he waited for his plan to run its course.

CHAPTER 4

It was 8:00 in the evening when Ed McDowell pulled up in front of the Lechner Apartments. It was a six-story structure, and Abigail had an apartment on the first floor. The building had first opened its doors to prospective rental tenants two years ago, and it was located in a respectable part of the city.

It was Ed's first date with Abigail, and he was taking her to dinner. Since he was new in town and wasn't familiar with the eating establishments, Conrad had mentioned a few of the better restaurants earlier in the day.

He decided he would suggest Italian dining, and if she were receptive, he would take her to Carbonellies. Conrad had told him it had the perfect atmosphere for two people to become further acquainted. The restaurant was elegant and impressive, and quaint enough to allow its patrons very comfortable and relaxed dinning. Of course, good food and plenty of wine would surely loosen Abigail up enough to talk freely.

Ed got out of the car holding a single, red rose in his hand. When he reached her door he rang the bell once. A moment later the door opened, and a smiling Abigail greeted him and said, "Hi, Ed."

His eyes quickly scanned her from head to foot, and he couldn't get over how lovely she looked standing there in a Jade, colored dress that caressed her shapely body. She was wearing a serpentine necklace that shone with the luster of 18 carat gold.

"Hi, Abigail," he finally said as if he had momentarily lost the ability to speak. "Oh, this is for you," and he handed her the rose, almost forgetting to give it to her. It made

him feel awkward and nervous as a schoolboy.

Sensing his initial nervousness, she gave him a warm, reassuring smile. "Oh, it's lovely, and how sweet of you, Ed. Come in while I put it in some water."

"Thank you," he said stepping into the small, open entrance way. From what he could see, the apartment appeared cheerful and tastefully decorated. He couldn't help noticing a large, ceramic statue of a giraffe placed off to the side of the entrance. "That's quite some statue," he commented.

"Yes, I just love it," she said as she placed her rose in a tall, slim vase. "I have several giraffe statues scattered throughout my apartment, but I'm afraid my bedroom is getting a little overrun."

"Any particular reason you're so fond of giraffes?" he asked. "Giraffes are not that common."

"When I was a little girl I was fascinated by their long necks. We lived near a small zoo, so my parents took me there now and then to see them. My dad kicked off my collection with a large, stuffed one I named Jiffy," and the fond memories of the past made her smile with a certain warmness even he could sense.

"Very interesting," said Ed. "To bad humans couldn't have their necks stretched like giraffes."

Abigail laughed hard. "Oh, my God, Ed, that's funny," and she laughed again. She picked up her purse and repeated, "That's so funny. Shall we leave?" she said still chuckling.

On the way to the car he said, "You look lovely, Abigail," and it was a sincere compliment.

"Thank you, Ed." She loved the compliment. She hadn't been out with anyone since her breakup with Conrad. She felt comfortable with Ed, and the evening looked extremely promising.

Once in the car, Ed said, "I'm rather new in the area so I may need your help with directions. I certainly wouldn't want to get lost."

"I'm not worried about that. After all, you already saved me once yesterday and I'm sure you're capable of handling almost any situation," and she looked at him smiling warmly.

"My destination, with your approval of course, is Carbonellies. I asked a neighbor that I met in the elevator of my condo if he could suggest a nice restaurant for dinner, and he emphatically said Carbonellies. "Do you like Italian?"

"It sounds fine. I love Italian," and she emphasized the word love.

"Have you ever been there?" he asked.

"Yes, I have."

Of course she had been there. And it's where Conrad wanted them to go tonight. She didn't have a clue, and she was so unsuspecting.

Though his acquaintance with Abigail was still in its infancy, he was beginning to realize that acting in a stage role and playing a part to willfully manipulate an individual's emotions were two different things. And playing the latter role was not going to be easy.

With the help of Abigail, Ed reached Carbonellies without making any wrong turns. It was a sole, brick building and nicely landscaped. A green, red and white canopy extended outward covering the entrance walkway. A doorman greeted them and wished them good dining as he opened the door.

Upon entering the dining area, Ed commented, "Thank you neighbor for an excellent choice." Abigail smiled saying, "It looks like you have a neighbor with good taste." As for himself, he was not at all surprised at the quaint elegance before him. After all, hadn't Conrad suggested coming here? He also knew restaurants of this caliber would be nothing new to Abigail considering her past relationship with Conrad.

One of the keys to Conrad's plan was to keep Abigail's expectations of Ed at a high level, and he was prepared financially to do whatever was necessary. He wanted her to believe Ed came from a background of good means even though he was a modest, young man trying to launch a rewarding career in acting. The more she thought and expected of him, the harder she would fall when he severed their relationship. Yes, the phony bitch had to fall hard and fast. She had to feel pain just as she had made him feel.

Having been previously instructed by Conrad, the maitre d seated Ed and Abigail in a private, quiet section of the dinning area.

Their table was situated on a raised terrace that overlooked a huge, stone fireplace. The area was dimly lit, with additional light being generated by lightly, scented candles that were encased in beautifully cut crystal glass in the center of each table. Ed loved the atmosphere and the fine dining which he was unaccustomed to. These were some of the benefits he would be receiving for playing his role.

When the waiter arrived, Ed asked, "Abigail, may I have the pleasure of ordering for you?"

"How sweet of you, Ed," she replied. "I truly love surprises." Ed looked at the waiter and said, "We would like to begin with Clams Casino and antipasto, followed by the Mediterranean Elegante and a bottle of Ruffino Classico, 1947.

When the waiter left, Abigail said, "The food here is excellent, and your selection was certainly interesting."

"Great, I'm a man who loves good food," and for a moment he studied her face illuminated by the soft candlelight. She was extremely attractive, her face full with cheeks lightly flushed with a rose, colored tint. She possessed a perfectly shaped nose that turned up slightly at the tip. Her lips were evenly balanced and full, and when she smiled her teeth glistened with the whiteness of freshly, fallen snow. Her hair was a deep auburn, and below her meticulous eyebrows framed within long, dark lashes were brown alert eyes that seemed to dance in the glow of the candlelight. It's a face, he thought, a face a man could easily fall in love with.

Then Ed said, "How is it a beautiful woman like you is not committed? There must be something wrong with the men in this area to let such a prize go unclaimed."

She lowered her head, looking down. Then she looked up at Ed and smiled. "I was in a relationship until just recently."

"I'm sorry. I hope I didn't offend you," he apologized.

"No apology necessary. It was for the best, and I'm glad it's over," and the tone of her voice gave every indication she was relieved.

Ed was anxious to find out what had happened between her and Conrad, but he didn't want to push the issue. Perhaps she would volunteer some information when she knew him better.

"How about you, Ed?" she asked. Are you involved with anyone?" and she couldn't believe how much she wanted him to say no.

Ed took a sip of water and moistened his lips. "I was. Actually, I had a short marriage. It just didn't work out," he said slowly rotating the water glass on the table.

"I'm sorry it didn't work out, Ed." As sincere as she was, she was delighted with the information. She hardly knew him, but she liked him a lot. There was a warmness his personality generated, and he appeared genuinely sincere with a calm demeanor, two qualities that attracted her.

The waiter arrived with the appetizers and offered the wine for Ed's approval before filling their glasses. "Enjoy," he said, and he gave them a smile as if he sensed they were in a new relationship.

Ed raised his glass and said, "I would like to propose a toast." Abigail smiled and raised her glass, curious as to what Ed was about to say.

"To a most lovely dinner companion, and hopefully this be the beginning of many more dinner engagements. And Ed continued the toast saying "and to all giraffes wherever they may be."

Abigail laughed. "I'll drink to that," she said as she raised her glass to gently brush against his. And she thought, He's also charming, and a man with a sense of humor. I like that.

"I'll bet the children at the hospital love you, Ed," she said remembering their conversation at the parking lot when they had first met, and he had mentioned that he also did volunteer work entertaining in the children's ward.

"Even if they don't, I still love them," and he winked his eye at her.

After Abigail had started her third glass of wine, she was starting to feel more relaxed. It also put her in a loquacious mood. With the wine glass in her hand, she looked affectionately into Ed's eyes. "You know, Ed, you're so different from Conrad," and she drank the remaining wine in the glass before putting it down.

It was the first time she mentioned his name. He hadn't expected to hear it so soon, and for a moment the name reverberated in his head.

"Conrad," he repeated, waiting for her to be more specific.

"I'm sorry. Of course you don't know who he is. He's the one I was recently involved with."

"I see. I hope it's a positive difference," he teased her.

"It is," and she reached over and squeezed his hand.

Our relationship is progressing favorably, he thought. The first contact between us has been made. Conrad will be pleased to hear about it.

Ed looked at Abigail, waiting for her to offer more about Conrad when the waiter arrived with their entrees and asked, "Is everything to your liking, Sir?"

"Yes, thank you. Everything is just fine," and what he was feeling went beyond the connotation of the word fine.

"Good, Bon Appetite," said the waiter, and he placed a large tray on his shoulder and walked out of the room.

Ed poured Abigail more wine filling her glass. She already had downed three glasses, and it was apparent the affect of the alcohol was making her loosen up enough to talk about Conrad. He wondered if she would continue making him the subject of their conversation.

She stared at Ed for a moment giving him the impression she was thinking, carefully planning her next words. Then she said, "He is such a foolish man. He has no one to blame but himself for blowing the relationship we enjoyed."

"I guess we sometimes don't realize we have a good thing until we lose it. Then unfortunately, it's to late and we come to regret it," Ed said in an understanding tone.

She was silent for a moment, staring into Ed's eyes that momentarily caused him to shift his eyes away. "Sometimes things happen that are a blessing in disguise even though you don't recognize it at the time. At least that's the way I see it."

"I understand. We all seem to have some imaginary idea of what we expect from life," he said.

She studied him again, staring into his eyes inquisitively. "After all, if I hadn't broken up with Conrad, I wouldn't be here with you."

"I can only take that as a compliment, Abigail. And I thank you." He could see she was becoming increasingly aggressive with her conversation. Was it the wine, or did she sincerely like him? Perhaps it was a combination of the two. Undoubtedly, he would know more as the evening progressed.

As they ate, Abigail monopolized the conversation expounding on Conrad's character and behavior. "He drinks to damn much. He got drunk in public a couple of times, and actually fell down. He embarrassed the hell out of me," and the recollection made her grimace. I may enjoy a few drinks, but I'm not a damn drunk." She took a sip of wine and continued. "It took a while to realize how self centered he was. It was always about what he wanted to do. Every time we were together he wanted to hop into bed. I mean I love sex, but give me a break," and she rolled her eyes. Then she asked, "Do you like sex, Ed?"

The unexpected question caught him by surprise, and it made him swallow. "Ugh, yes, of course I do." He hesitated for a moment, and he said, "I guess it depends on whom I'm with."

Abigail smiled. "I can understand that. We all need a turn on." She picked up her wine glass and drank it dry. "I'm sorry, Ed, I didn't mean to monopolize the conversation," she apologized.

"No, no, it's okay. It's good to get it off your chest. Actually, I'm pleased you feel comfortable enough to share your feelings with me. I'm a good listener."

"You're a sweetheart. We haven't known each other long, but from where I'm sitting I think whoever let you get away was a fool."

Ed smiled and said, "My sentiments exactly," and they both laughed.

Then Abigail became serious. "It's funny, I think back to when Conrad and I shared many laughs. Then the more I got to know him, the moments of laughter became less and less. He would always tell me he was going to put me on a pedestal. I would reply, "Yeah, I hope it's not shaped like a penis, and he would always burst into laughter."

The remark made Ed laugh. "That's a first for me, Abigail. Tell me, did you ever let him know how you felt?" and his curiosity was aroused.

"Most of the time I did, but it all went over his head. It seemed he had a buzz on most of the time. It's his loss," and she demonstrated no apparent remorse regarding the broken relationship. "I mean, I didn't want to be with a drunk for the rest of my life. Of course he would never admit it. When I had had enough, I called him and told him it was over. When he asked me why, all I said was you should know, and I gave no further explanation."

His first impression was he thought it was a cruel way to break off a relationship. It seemed to him that Conrad deserved some sort of explanation, but who was he to judge her. Although he had only Abigail's interpretation of the relationship, it gave him some insight to the events that had transpired between them. Now if he could only get Conrad to reveal his version, he would be in a better position to draw his own conclusion. I want the whole picture, he thought.

When they were finished with dinner and Ed had paid the check, Abigail said, "Thank you for dinner, Ed. I'm sorry I monopolized the evening with my tale of woe. I guess the wine got to me. Next time you can tell me all about yourself, and I promise to give you my undivided attention. There will be a next time?" she asked, raising her eyebrows anticipating an answer of yes.

"Absolutely," he assured her. "Absolutely," he repeated, and her eagerness to go out with him pleased him far beyond a successful commitment to the part he was playing.

"I really want to know all about Ed McDowell," and she took hold of his arm as they walked out of the restaurant.

When Ed opened the car door for her, she slid over on the seat so she would be close to him. After he was seated, she placed her arm around his. She looked at him adoringly through eyes glazed from the consumption of wine. "I'm not telling you how to get me home. I want to see if you remember. Don't drive into the curbing now," and she giggled like a schoolgirl.

"Well, if I get lost I can always take you to my apartment."

"Is that a promise? I don't like broken promises," and she tugged on his arm.

"It's a promise."

"Good-boy," she said, and she rested her head against his shoulder.

When they reached the entrance to her apartment, Abigail turned to Ed and looked into his eyes. "Would you like to come in?" and her eyes were burning with passion. Before he could answer, she stepped forward and pressed her lips hard against his. A moment later he could fell her hot tongue caressing the walls of his mouth.

"Please come in and make love to me," she pleaded with her breath quickening. Her words quickly sent a jolt of excitement throughout his body as if someone had injected him with a needle. Her driving passion caused her to fumble with the key before she opened the door.

As soon as they entered the apartment, she took him by the hand and quickly led him into the bedroom. She undressed herself hurriedly and was naked in an instant, her clothing discarded recklessly on the floor. She was standing in a beam of moonlight that streaked through the bedroom window. He was naked to the waist, and when he saw her he savored the sight of her naked body embellished by the moonlight. Her breasts were full, round, and extremely firm with large, protruding nipples. In fierce passion he began fondling them with his hands, and then with his mouth, moving his tongue with quick, flickering strokes on her nipples and around the surface of her breasts, making her moan. They were kissing passionately, clinging and breathing heavily.

"Do you like what you see?" she asked with her mouth against his ear.

"Yes, yes," he answered approvingly, never before having felt such an exhilarating response to any woman.

Then she pulled him wildly against her making them topple onto the bed. Immediately she was tugging and pulling at his clothing, desperately trying to remove it. When all of his clothing was removed, she grew more anxious. When he was naked she could feel his muscular, athletic body and his hard, male organ pressing against her.

"Stick it in me, Ed," she begged. "Oh, stick it in me," she repeated impatient to feel him. When he penetrated her, she moaned with pleasure. "That's good. That's so good," she said, and her hands were rapidly sledding over the muscles of his back. Infused with desire, he began thrusting her hard and deep, and it was the kind of sex that pleased her. He was making her feel good with every thrust, and she was rocking and moving with him, gyrating her hips rhythmically. Molten shafts of sensation were running down her stomach to her legs. She was beginning to reach climax, and her body was reacting with quick, shuddering spasms.

"Come on, baby, come on, baby," she moaned, and when she peaked at orgasm she screamed intensely with the moment exploding all around her.

The excitement of her orgasm made him thrust her harder and faster until the blood was pounding in his temples.

"Come on, baby, come on," she coaxed him sensing he was about to explode within her. Moments later he ejaculated into her, and soon after she could feel the weight of his spent body on her.

"That was wonderful, so wonderful," she said. Then she kissed him as if to pay tribute to his sexual prowess. "I never felt so good. We definitely have to do this again. Oh, yes," her voice filled with excitement. Ed looked at her and nodded approvingly. "You're beautiful, Abigail."

As they rested their spent bodies from the torrid, sexual excitement, he looked at her lying on her back with her eyes closed and savored the sight of her beautiful body, struggling to tame the urge to take her again. It made him wonder what had just happened. Had he acted out a role he was hired to play, or did he experience something he really wanted to do? One thing was certain. He loved being with her, and he felt wonderful.

CHAPTER 5

It was noon when Ed returned to his apartment after spending the night with Abigail. It had been a great evening and night, and a pleasurable chain of events he definitely had not expected to experience this early in their relationship.

Shortly after Ed's return to his condo, Conrad was ringing his telephone. "This is Ed," he answered speculating Conrad would be on the other end.

"Christ, Ed, where the hell have you been? I've been calling you all morning," and the tone of his voice assured Ed he was annoyed.

"Oh, I guess I had too much wine last night, so I got up early and walked outside for awhile. Then I decided to have breakfast out. I feel better now."

"Is that right, Ed? How do you think Abigail feels?" and he eagerly waited for Ed's answer.

"I,"… and Ed hesitated for a moment, Conrad's question catching him by surprise. "I hope she feels okay. I haven't talked to her since last night," and he had no intention of telling him they had spent the night together. He could sense Conrad still had feelings for Abigail, regardless of what he was doing and saying. He elected to spare him of any additional hurt at this time.

"So, what you're saying is you both had to much to drink last night at dinner. Ed, you didn't screw her did you?"

"No, no, we didn't have sex," and he didn't like lying. "Just a good dinner, some laughs, and a lot of wine. But I'm taking her out again. Good news, buddy?"

"Good news, Ed. Tell me, did she say anything about why she left me?"

Another fragile question, thought Ed. He wasn't quite sure how he should answer it even though he had anticipated Conrad asking it. He would have to step around the absolute truth, another attempt to spare his friend from being hurt. "She did mention a couple of things."

"Like what?" Conrad was quick to ask.

"Well, she said at times you drink too much."

"That bitch," he snapped. "She drinks more than I do. Then when she gets high, she wants to screw everybody. Tell me Ed, you sure she didn't come on to you?" and he was upset.

He wanted to say yes, but he couldn't bring himself to say it. "She was a little loose buddy, but it was only our first date. Perhaps she will try something next time," and Ed wondered if what Conrad said was true. If it were, he obviously still had loved her no matter what faults or undesirable behavior she had manifested during their time together.

"What else did she say?" Then he quickly said, "Never mind. I don't really care what she said. The bitch is a total liar, Ed. Just keep on doing whatever it takes to win her over. Then we will go for the kill," and he said the word kill with passion.

"Sure, buddy," said Ed, "Whatever you want. You call the shots."

"That's right, Ed. I do call the shots, and don't forget it," and he deliberately repeated Ed's words.

"I'll call you after our next date, buddy."

"You do that, Ed. Meantime I have something important to do, real important," and he hung up.

"I wonder what he meant by real important," Ed thought aloud. And he wondered if it had anything to do with Abigail or him. His thoughts started drifting to Abigail. He missed her already, and it was only early afternoon Sunday. He had only been away from her for a couple of hours, and he couldn't understand why he felt the way he did. There was no question he thought she was beautiful, and he enjoyed talking to her. And of course, there was the great night in bed. He hadn't been intimate with a girl since he and Shelly had divorced. He decided he would reconcile himself to the fact it was a combination of things, and that further speculation wasn't necessary. The truth was he missed her.

He poured himself a glass of orange juice and started pacing in the living room, glancing at the telephone, debating whether or not he should call, as he paced. A moment later, he capitulated to his desire to call and picked up the phone and dialed Abigail's number.

"This is Abigail," she said softly.

He liked the sound of her voice. "Hi, Abigail, it's Ed."

"What a nice surprise. I wasn't expecting you to call."

"To tell the truth, I wasn't either."

She laughed. "Then why did you, silly boy?"

"To put it simply, I miss you."

"You do? How nice. Then I'll let you do something about it. I'm here, all by myself," she said in an upbeat tone.

"You sure I'm not being a pest?"

"Not at all," she said. "You can be a wasp and sting me anytime," and her voice was sexy.

"Great, I'll have my stinger ready, so beware."

"I think I can handle it. After that wasp messes with me, I can assure you its stinger will be limp," and she laughed. "Get my drift, Ed?"

"Oh, I get your drift all right." He loved her responses. They were quick and often witty. It was a quality of hers he loved.

"I'll be there in less than an hour. Do you think you can handle the wait?"

"It won't be easy, but I know I'll be rewarded for my patience. And I'll give you a hint. I'm not looking for a money reward. Need I say more?" and she was enjoying the conversation.

"Absolutely not, and I'll be there in a flash."

"I'll leave the door open, Ed, just in case I'm in the shower. See you soon."

"Bye, baby," and he hung up the phone. He would be seeing her again, and he was actually excited. It made him take a couple of deep breathes to slow his pulse. Then he showered, dressed in fresh clothing and splashed on his most expensive cologne. He had to smell good for her. And when he left the condo, he was whistling.

When he arrived at Abigail's apartment, he knocked on the door. When she didn't answer, he turned the doorknob and opened the door slowly, calling out, "Abigail, it's Ed." Since there was no response, he headed for the bathroom. When he reached the doorway he could see her naked body through the smoked glass of the shower wall, and he called out over the sound of the running water, "Abigail, its Ed."

"Come in, Ed, the water's great," and he walked to the shower door. She immediately opened it and took hold of his hand, and smiling seductively, led him in. In a fraction he clutched her body and pulled her against him. He started kissing her passionately, the warm water streaming down on them drenching his clothing. And as the shower walls started to steam up, he couldn't help but think he was acting in the greatest role he ever had to play, and opposite a leading lady quite different than any other he had dealt with.

CHAPTER 6

Conrad was seated in the gazebo which over looked the pool and the surrounding garden area. Clutched in his hand was the morning newspaper. On the side table was a glass of vodka and orange juice. Reading the newspaper and drinking vodka had become a morning routine since his breakup with Abigail McCloud. He had voluntarily scratched his obligation to work at his father's business citing mental anguish and undue stress conditions he believed rendered him useless. Of course, it was his diagnosis, and one that he chose not to address with medical treatment.

As he started to read the headlines, his mother approached him. She had a stern expression on her face as she seated herself next to him. He had seen the same facial expression before, and inevitably, it meant some kind of tirade was forth coming. Past experience made him well aware of the fact his mother believed that her lectures, or conversations as she referred to it, were constructive and for the benefit of his welfare. But he didn't see it that way, and most of the time he construed his mother's lectures as a pain in the ass.

She promptly folded the newspaper in half and pushed it away, for there could be no distractions when she talked. "Conrad, this irresponsible behavior must stop. You simply must get over Abigail."

He stared at the empty glass, then at his mother. "You don't understand, mother. You just don't understand."

"I do, Conrad. You have to let go and start over. You're not the first young man to have his heart broken, and you won't be the last. There are plenty of respectable, young ladies out there, but it will require an effort on your part to make their acquaintance," and her words were stern and unwavering.

"I'm not ready for another relationship, mother. I need more time. Please try to understand," he pleaded.

"Your father and I are trying to understand, believe me we are," and she rolled her eyes trying not to run out of patience. "Perhaps going back to work will help you forget her. You need to concentrate on something else." She stared at him momentarily and then said, "Why don't you spend some time with Dr. Drier. I'm sure he can help you see things differently. He has a fine reputation."

"Damn it, mother, I don't need a shrink. I can handle this myself. I just need more time," and she was wearing down his patience. He just couldn't handle a lengthy conversation. The more she spoke, the more repugnant her words became.

"Well," she said with indignation. "Suit yourself, Conrad. But your father and I will not tolerate this kind of conduct from you much longer. Do you understand? You need to get a life."

"Fine, mother," and he turned away and took hold of the newspaper and waited for her to leave.

"Pathetic boy," she grumbled, and she walked away briskly, disturbed by his dismissal.

Conrad got up from the chair and walked over to the railing of the gazebo facing the woods. He inhaled deeply for a moment filling his lungs with the fresh, morning air. Then he said, "It's your fault, Abigail, you miserable phony. You will get yours, you treacherous bitch," and the thought gave him some consolation. Yes, Ed was working on it, and he could depend on him to finish the job.

He opened the newspaper to the front page, and the headlines of one of the articles caught his attention. It read, ERICA HOLLIS WINS MISS FAIRFIELD COUNTY PAGEANT.

Her photograph accompanied the article. She looked so familiar, this Erica Hollis. And her name definitely rang a bell. He thought harder. Of course he knew who she was. She was in some of his classes in high school his senior year. She was the beauty who caused the boys to get an erection by just walking by. He should have recognized her instantly. What was the matter with him?

Nothing was the matter with him. It was Abigail. Yes, the bitch had messed up his mind. But she wouldn't mess it up anymore. Like he had told himself before, he had to go on a mission like Ed, and he would start with Erica Hollis.

After reading the article on Erica Hollis, Conrad knew she was a customer service representative for Mercer-Bennett a very well known authorized dealership for Mercedes-Benz. He would pretend he was interested in purchasing a new Mercedes, and after inspecting a few models, he would ask to see his former classmate, Erica. With all the hype over her recent crowning, it would be perfectly understandable. She should remember him; after all, throughout his high school years he had been regarded as dashingly handsome. And the consensus had been that he would inevitably be paired with a beautiful woman. Now, he could live up to the prophecy.

Shortly after noon, Conrad was at the Mercer-Bennett dealership. When he exited his Trans-Am, a young salesman approached him. "Hi, my name is Matt Bowers," and he offered his hand.

Conrad took hold of it and they engaged in a handshake. "I'm Conrad Hill."

"I'm pleased to meet you, Conrad. How may I help you today?"

"Actually, I'm just browsing. But if I see anything I'm interested in, I'll let you know."

"I see," the young salesman said, concealing his initial disappointment of not having a hot prospect. "I'll leave you my card in case you have any questions," and he handed him his card and walked away in the direction of a vehicle that had just pulled into the parking lot.

"Not aggressive enough," Conrad quickly evaluated him. It was just as well. He really wasn't in the mood to hear any high-pressure sales pitch. He was here to see Erica Hollis.

After walking around in the pretense of inspecting some vehicles, he went into the showroom and approached the receptionist. "Good afternoon, I'm Conrad Hill, and I would like to see Erica Hollis."

"Is she expecting you, sir?"

"For the last seven years," he answered with a grin.

The receptionist stared at him, and then her lips broke into a soft smile. "You're kidding, right?"

"Yes, I'm kidding," and he returned a gracious smile. "I'm an old friend. I would really appreciate seeing her. I'm sure a woman as charming as you could arrange it."

"Sure, Mr. Hill," said the receptionist. Let me see if she is available." She picked up the phone and a moment later said, "She'll see you, Mr. Hill. Just go down that hall and her office is the last one on the left."

"Thank you so much, Ms. ...?"

"Michelle Loft," she answered smiling.

"Thank you so much, Michelle Loft," and he winked his eye.

Erica was standing in the hallway by her office door when Conrad approached.

"Hi, Conrad, I don't believe I'm seeing you here," and she was pleased to see him. "How long has it been, about seven years?"

"About that, and it's great to see you, Erica," and he gave her a hug.

"What brings you to our dealership?" she asked making a gesture with her hand toward her office. When they were in her office she said, "Please, Conrad, have a seat."

"Actually, I came to see you. I saw your picture in the newspaper. May I offer my belated congratulations on winning the Miss Fairfield County Pageant?"

"Thank you. I'm flattered you came to congratulate me in person, especially after not seeing each other in seven years." She chuckled and said, Actually, I remember having a crush on you in high school. But I was just one of many."

"Is that right? I guess I was a complete fool not to pick up on it. I guess there was something wrong with my radar," and he shook his head acknowledging regret.

"Well, how is your radar these days?" she teased.

"It's much better. I was just reading the newspaper enjoying a cup of coffee, when all of a sudden this sonic alarm went off in my head. It nearly took my head off, so who am I to ignore something like that. Isn't it amazing after all these years?" He stared at her for a moment. She hardly looked any different after seven years. She still had a hell of a figure, and her blonde hair was still down to her shoulders, curling up at the ends. Her beautiful, azure eyes sparkled more than he remembered, and her lips were voluptuous and inviting. She was a knockout that would arouse any man's genitals.

"So tell me, Erica, how have you managed to stay single all these years? I'm assuming you are after being crowned, MISS FAIRFIELD COUNTY."

I am now. I previously had an unsuccessful marriage. I thought I was going to have a life long commitment, but it didn't work out that way," she said shrugging her shoulders.

"Life's a bitch, isn't it? I refer to it as a predator and we people are its prey," and his facial expression was serious.

"That's an interesting concept, Conrad. Where did you read it?"

"I didn't. It's an original."

"I'm impressed, even though it conveys pessimism. Are you a pessimist? Of course he was, but he would never let her know it.

"Maybe at times I am. Isn't this true of everyone, Erica, or are you an eternal optimist?"

"Eternal no, but most of the time I guess," and before she could say another word the phone rang.

"This is Erica. Sure, Michelle, I'll see them in a minute. Conrad, I have to see some customers. Let me give you my card," and she quickly wrote her home phone number on it. "Please give me a call.

Perhaps we can get together some evening and catch up on things," and she gave him a hug.

"Sure, Erica, I'd like that, and rest assured I'll call real soon. Take care now."

It was exactly what he had wanted, the beginning of a relationship with the beautiful Erica Hollis, the aspiring beauty queen. And the kickoff seemed so remarkably easy. It was a good omen he would be able to carry out his plan to a successful finale. To him, a conclusion that could only have a medicinal effect on relieving the pain he was still feeling that had been inflicted on him by the phony bitch, Abigail McCloud.

CHAPTER 7

*I*t was a hot, humid August morning when Ed McDowell arrived at the Fairfield Memorial Hospital. He had decided it was time for Abigail to witness one of his performances as "Laffy" the clown for the entertainment of the sick children. In doing so, it would give her a chance to see the other side of his character and personality. His primary motive was to enhance her feelings for him and their relationship by letting her see his natural compassion and gentleness when he was working with the children. He was not at all concerned about his performance, because he genuinely loved seeing young people smile and laugh. It always gave him undeniable pleasure to think he could make them forget their pain and suffering even for a short time.

Their first date had been perfect right to the end, which had culminated with them spending the entire night together. Not to mention the following afternoon, which seemed to be an extension of the previous evening, most of which was spent in the sack. Now he must continue to impress her. After all, he had an obligation to Conrad. He had given his old military buddy his word, and there had been no rules against enjoying his part.

He had an eleven in the morning appointment with Jennifer Sweet, Vice President of Public Relations at the hospital. She had expressed an extreme interest in what he had to offer during their phone conversation. If the past were any indication of the future, she would jump at the opportunity to have him perform for the children.

Her office was on the eighth floor, and when he got off the elevator one side of the wall was glass from the ceiling to the floor. It provided a beautiful view of the downtown area and the suburbs that flowed into the countryside. After pausing momentarily to savor the view, he headed for the reception area.

"Hi, I'm Ed McDowell. Jennifer Sweet is expecting me. I have an eleven o'clock appointment," he informed the receptionist.

"Yes, Mr. McDowell, she is expecting you. One moment, please," and she activated the intercom. "You may go right in, Mr. McDowell."

"Thank you," and when he entered the office Jennifer was standing behind her desk. "Hello, Mr. McDowell, and she extended her hand reaching across the desk. "I'm Jennifer Sweet."

"Pleased to meet you," and he shook her hand.

"Please sit down."

She didn't look anything like he had imagined. He was expecting someone short and stout and extremely academic, perhaps with short hair and glasses. Instead, she was young, tall and slender. She emanated a glowing, amorous quality, and it was obvious she was an extrovert. He liked her.

"So, Mr. McDowell, you want to entertain in our children's ward."

"Please, call me Ed," he interjected.

"All right," she said and smiled. "I think it's wonderful that you want to volunteer your time for the entertainment of sick children," she continued. "Can you briefly tell me about your character Laffy the clown?"

"Yes, Ms. Sweet."

"Now it's my turn," she interrupted. "You may call me Jennifer."

"I will, thank you," and he gave her a warm smile. "I started doing Laffy the clown about a year ago. He's a character who experiences uncontrollable laughter. I find nothing makes children laugh more than when they see someone else laugh excessively coupled with some funny antics. I guess I'm utilizing the philosophy laughter is contagious along with the belief it's conducive to good health."

She was listening intently and her eyes reflected admiration as he spoke. When he paused to shift himself in the chair, she said, "Your character sounds great, Ed. I concur with your laughter philosophy. I think it's important for the children to laugh. I don't think anyone can have enough laughter in their life," and it made him feel good that she agreed.

"I also have a hand puppet which I include in my routine. It's a mirror image of Laffy. I call him little Laffy. The children get a kick out of it."

Jennifer brought her hands together and laughed. "That sounds just great, Ed. I'm looking forward to seeing the show myself. I'll definitely have to arrange my schedules so there is no conflict," and he was flattered she wanted to attend.

"My availability between nine and five is quite flexible. Perhaps it won't be difficult at all," Ed told her.

"I can tell you up front it can be as early as next week. We usually like to arrange any activities involving the children between eleven and twelve in the morning, and three and four in the afternoon. It's the time that least conflicts with their treatments. If that presents a problem for you, we can try to arrange something else."

"No, that time seems to be just fine."

"I'll check with my secretary and get back to you when we have the first available day," and she walked up to him offering her hand.

"Thank you so much, Ed, and I appreciate your generous offer. I know the children will be delighted."

"The pleasure is mine, Jennifer. I just want to help. You see, just being with the children in itself is rewarding to me."

As Ed was leaving the office he paused in the doorway and said, "Take care now. I'll be looking forward to your call." Oh yes, he liked her. She was warm, and he suspected she was a very giving person. He liked that quality.

Now that he was a shoo-in to perform, he would call Abigail and let her know. He was excited and anxious to perform.

Later that evening he was on the phone with Abigail. "I'm going to be performing at the Fairfield Memorial Hospital in the children's ward next week. I met with the Public Relations director earlier today, Abigail," and his voice was upbeat.

"Good for you, Ed. What did you tell him?"

"I had previously told her on the phone that I was pursuing an acting career, and that on occasion I did charity work entertaining children at various hospitals.

"You said her," she interjected. "Then the director is a woman? What did you do, charm her into letting you perform?" she teased.

"Absolutely," he countered, "and it worked well. I didn't realize I had such persuasive power."

"That's not the only talent you have, Ed, if you know what I mean."

"I think I know what you mean, Abigail," and he was laughing.

"Tell you what, Ed, why don't you plan on having dinner with me Saturday night at my place. I'll do the cooking, and I promise to give you a dessert you'll just love. Trust me on this one."

"Sounds great, but only if you promise to see my performance at the hospital," he bargained. "Say yes, I really don't want to miss dessert."

"Deal, Ed McDowell. I'm very curious to see how you perform in other areas." Then she said, "I think I'll refer to you as the remarkable performer."

He laughed. "You're quite the performer yourself."

"How nice of you to say so," she said. Your dessert just got better."

"Wow, I'm getting more excited by the minute," and he wasn't kidding.

"You should be. That's my intent."

"With those words, Ms. McCloud, I will bid thee farewell. I can't take the excitement any longer," he teased.

"Okay, Ed. I'll just sit here with my giraffe's. Bye, see you Saturday. Dinner will be ready at seven."

"That's great," and he hung up. Another great weekend was shaping up. He would get to taste her cooking, and inevitably, have a dynamic time with her in bed.

Ed was at the Lechner Apartments at six forty five in the evening. Earlier, he had stopped at the mall to see if he could find a statue of a giraffe to give to Abigail as a gift. He had been fortunate enough to find one about eight inches tall, carved from Teakwood with amazing details. He was outwardly pleased and even more so when the saleslady asked if he would like it gift-wrapped. After choosing an appropriate paper with an African motif, he left the store with his treasure under his arm. And he hoped the gift would be another strategic move in helping to win her over.

When he rang the doorbell, he held the box behind him.

"Hi, Ed," Abigail greeted him as she swung the door open. And when he stepped in, she planted a long, passionate kiss on his lips.

"Here, this is for you," he said handing her the box.

"Oh my, a surprise, and it's not even Christmas." She was visibly surprised. "That's so sweet of you, Ed. Can I open it now? I just love surprises," and she was smiling and as excited as a child.

"After the wonderful greeting I just received, absolutely," and he was hoping she would like it.

She quickly opened the package, and when she saw the giraffe, her facial expression changed from curious to delight. "I love it, Ed. I don't have anything in Teakwood. I love you, for giving it to me," and she threw her arms around him and kissed him repeatedly.

It was the first time either one of them had said the words I love you. He construed them as having the connotation could be in the process of being primed for their relationship to the next level. A much more serious level, at least as far as she was concerned. And he wondered if he should use the L word, lightly of course, too. It would surely solidify their relationship. Perhaps the appropriate time was now. After all, the goal was to capture her heart and then break it. It was what Conrad wanted. He decided to say, "I loved giving it to you, Abigail," and they kissed again.

She was beaming. It had been a long time since he had seen a girl so happy. She was an emotional being. He had seen and felt it when she made love. Every time they conversed there was always feeling and expression in her words and movements. And he couldn't help but wonder how much more difficult it would be for her to handle and adjust to a sudden, unexpected broken relationship. He also knew he would have to try to put the thought out of his mind, at least for now. It would be difficult enough knowing he was to be the heavy when the time came.

"Dinner will be ready in a bit, my darling," and she looked at him admiringly.

"It smells great, and it's obvious we are eating Italian."

"Right, you are; spaghetti, meatballs, garlic bread, and red wine, of course."

He could see she was anxious to please him, and he was convinced she would in more ways than one.

"Tell me, Abigail, does this restaurant serve topless?"

"It could," she chuckled, "but it's not. You would be so absorbed with the breasts of the waitress that you wouldn't be able to concentrate on the excellent food."

"Darn, I'll settle for the food now. Maybe I'll get lucky later."

"Sex maniac," and she winked her eye.

He laughed, enjoying the conversation, and he followed her with his eyes as she finalized the preparation of the meal.

"Okay, my darling, it's time to eat. Place your handsome butt on the chair." She had set the table with her best china, glassware and silver. Two long, white candles adorned the table. It was the first time she had cooked for him, and she wanted it to be romantic. When the food was on the table, she lit the candles and filled the glasses with wine.

"Before we eat, I'd like to propose a toast," said Ed, and the words brought a smile to her lips. Their glasses came together with a clink and he said, "To a long lasting relationship, and my sincerest thanks to the chef."

"I'll drink to that, and I hope the chef is worthy of the toast."

"This is good, Abigail," he said after his first swallow. Where did you learn to cook Italian?" The taste exceeded his expectations.

"My grandmother was Italian. My mom's maiden name is Conti. My sauce is her recipe. See, I'm full of surprises."

"I'm impressed. With the name McCloud, I didn't anticipate any Italian blood."

"That's understandable, Ed. Enough about me, let's hear about Ed. I really know very little about the man I'm getting to love more and more. So come on, let's hear it," gesturing with her hand for him to speak.

Just as he was about to speak, the phone rang. "Saved by the bell," and she picked up the phone on the counter. "Hello, this is Abigail. Hello," she repeated. "Okay, don't speak," and she hung up. Seconds later it rang again. "Hello, Abigail speaking." Then she heard heavy breathing followed by a high-pitched, wailing sound. She looked at Ed and grimaced as the wailing sound continued. Then it ceased and the line went to a dial tone.

"What is it, Abigail?" Ed asked concerned.

"I don't know. It was strange. The first time there wasn't a sound, but with the second call I could hear heavy breathing followed by a high-pitched, wailing sound. It was really weird," she said frowning.

"Probably some kids playing around with the telephone," he concluded. "If it rings again, I'll answer it," he offered.

"I'll let you. Now, please tell me about Ed."

He smiled. "There isn't a whole lot to tell, just some boring basics."

"Boring or not, I want to hear them," she persisted.

"On January seventh, the greatest thing in the world happened. I was born," and he looked straight into her eyes.

She laughed, "Cute, real cute, and such a dramatic beginning. Please continue."

"When I was three, I started walking," and he made her laugh again. "When I was four I painted the family dog white," he continued, "and when I was five, I was toilet trained," and she was laughing incessantly. "Please stop, you're giving me a stomach ache and I can't eat."

"Wait, there's more. When I was eight, I drove the family car to school by myself."

"Stop, Ed," she begged holding onto her stomach. Her eyes were tearing from the laughter. "You win. You don't have to tell me about yourself anymore. At least not for now," and she dried her eyes with a tissue.

He really didn't want to get into the serious part of his life, at least not for the present time. She already cared a great deal for him with the limited information she had. If she persisted again, he would deal with it then.

When they finished with the meal Ed said, "That was great, Abigail. Thank, you," and he was sincere with his compliment. "Can I help you clean up?"

"Sure, the sooner we do, the sooner the dessert will be available."

He was still speculating as to what exactly it would be. He had an inkling she was involved personally based on the phone conversation he had had with her when she brought up the topic.

When the dishes were washed and dried, and the kitchen tidied up, Abigail said, "You sit here in the den and I'll see what I can do about dessert. Please remain here until I call you," and she kissed him on the forehead.

"Sure, Abigail," and he liked the suspense.

"It won't be long," she promised.

Ten minutes had elapsed, and with him being anxious, made it appear a lot longer. A moment later he heard her say, "Okay, Ed, come in the bedroom."

It was the invitation he was waiting for. Dessert would be in the bedroom, and excitement flowed throughout his body. He walked hurriedly to the bedroom and stopped in the doorway. When he saw her, his lips separated and his pulse started to quicken. She was naked, lying on her side on the bed, looking at him seductively. Each nipple was buried under a mound of thick, whip cream, and the third mound covered her genitals.

"My, God," he uttered softly, and he became motionless, staring at and savoring the beautiful sight of her naked body.

"Well, are you going to stand there or come and take your dessert?" she asked anxious and full of desire.

In a fraction he was no longer motionless, and was licking her neck and shoulders with his tongue, flicking it quickly in little, piston like strokes arousing her sexual passion. His tongue journeyed into her cleavage, and then onto her breasts. She moaned and panted when he sucked the whip cream from her nipples. As his passion increased he was more determined than ever to make her experience a new level of sexual pleasure. When he started licking the whip cream from her genitals, she moaned deeply and started running her fingers through his hair.

"Don't stop, Ed. Please don't stop," she begged repeatedly, her body rapidly approaching orgasm. He was relentless in his attempt to please her. As her body was being ravaged with sexual pleasure her tongue was moving wildly back and forth across her lips and she wished the rapture would never end. Her head was rocking side to side and when her body responded with an orgasm, he could feel her body jerk with orgasmic spasms. "Oh, my God," she screamed, her chest rising up and down from her heavy breathing. "It was unbelievable," she said continuing to express her orgasmic ecstasy. "I love you, my darling. I love you," and she held him tightly, her pulse still racing.

A moment later she said, "Your turn, my darling," and she undressed him. "I told you dessert was special." She took hold of his organ and covered it with whip cream. Then she flicked her tongue over his body as he had done to her, arousing him until his organ was rock hard. As she lovingly licked the whip cream from his male member he closed his eyes, and when she made his organ burst into orgasm he experienced the most beautiful moment of ecstasy.

Later, after a brief rest, Abigail said, "Let's do it again, Ed," and she started to tickle him.

"Okay, you win," he said remembering the last time she tickled him relentlessly. They made passionate love again. After they were finished, Abigail held his hand and said smiling, "Guess what I want?"

He looked at her and said, "You're insatiable, Abigail."

"Okay, I'll let you rest for a while," and she stroked his forehead and cheeks with her hand. He smiled at her and then closed his eyes.

— ✴ —

CHAPTER 8

Three days after Ed had dinner at Abigail's apartment, he received a phone call from Jennifer Sweet's secretary.

"Mr. McDowell, Ms. Sweet would like to know if you would be available to perform at two in the afternoon this Friday?"

"Tell her Friday is fine. And thank you for giving me the opportunity to entertain the children," he said with gratitude.

"Thank you, Mr. McDowell. I'll convey the message to Ms. Sweet. You have a nice day now," and she hung up.

So he was performing Friday. That gave him two days to make sure all of his props were in order. Being an amateur ventriloquist, he always took time to practice his ventriloquism before he performed with his look a like dummy, Laffy. While he practiced, he would stand before a mirror so he could see how he looked in front of an audience. His goal always was to improve his act so he could deliver the most entertaining show possible for the benefit of the children. They must laugh, and they must laugh a great deal. They must forget where they are and become absorbed with the comedy. Only then would he feel he accomplished something, and it would be more rewarding than if he had performed in a Broadway show.

He wondered if Abigail would attend, and if Jennifer Sweet would be there after she gave every indication she would arrange her work schedule so it wouldn't conflict with his performance. He surprised himself with how much he cared whether or not they would attend.

Ed was awakened by the telephone the night before his scheduled performance. When he reached to answer it, he noticed the dial on the clock next to his bed read twelve midnight. "Who could be calling at midnight?" he thought.

"Hello," he said into the receiver, unable to stop yawning.

"Ed, Abigail. I know it's late, but I just had another one of those weird phone calls," her voice distressed.

"Was there any conversation?" he asked, his body suddenly awakened.

"No, just the heavy breathing; and then that weird, wailing sound. It's starting to spook me, Ed."

"Stay calm, Abigail," Ed tried to relax her. "My first impression is some clown has your number, probably by accident, and is playing games with you. Since they refrain from talking to you, I don't think you have anything to worry about. Could even be kids."

"You think so?" she asked looking for assurance.

"Good possibility." Then he thought for a moment. "Do you have a whistle in your apartment?"

"No, I don't. Why do you ask, Ed?"

"If they should call again, you could blow it really hard into the phone. I understand it can do a job on someone's ear," and he chuckled. "The varmint will probably never call you again."

"I wish I had one. I'll be sure to purchase one tomorrow. Thanks for the information Ed. I feel better now after talking to you. I wish you were here holding me, my darling," she hankered.

"I wish I were there too. Why don't you leave the phone off the hook for the remainder of the night? It might discourage the low-life from calling you anymore," and he hoped his suggestion would pacify her.

"Okay, Ed. I'll do that. I love you."

"I'll see you at the hospital tomorrow. Sleep tight and don't worry."

He didn't want her to worry, but he was concerned. He was unsure if someone was deliberately trying to frighten her or if it was a genuine prank. He knew nothing about her circle of friends, so he couldn't even speculate if an unhappy friend or acquaintance was responsible. It could be anyone.

He had thought enough, and he had to perform tomorrow. Now he had to rest. He rolled over on his side and fell asleep.

Ed arrived at the Fairfield Memorial Hospital an hour before his scheduled performance time. He hadn't performed in sometime, and he was looking forward to it.

Natalie West, assistant to Jennifer Sweet, had the assignment to see Ed had everything he needed to deliver his routine. "You can change your clothing in this room, Mr. McDowell, and when you're ready, I'll take you to the children's ward. If there's anything else you need, please don't hesitate to ask."

"Thank you, Ms. West. You're very kind."

After changing into an outfit of loose, yellow pants with black strips, and a bright blue, puffy sleeved shirt, Ed prepared his character's face. When it was completed, Laffy the clown had a white face, huge red lips, black streaks around the eyes, and a large, red nose that resembled a light bulb. On his feet were very large, black shoes that turned up at the toes. His dummy was a small replica of himself.

He was ready to go, and when he approached Ms. West he said, "How do I look?" expecting her approval.

Her face lit up with an expression of amazement. "You look fantastic, Mr. McDowell," and she was smiling approvingly.

"Please, call me, Ed."

"Sure, Ed," she replied. The children are just going to love you."

"I sure hope so. Shall we go?"

"Of course, and we have to take the elevator to the third floor."

"Are you planning to take in the show?" he asked her as they entered the elevator.

"Yes, I am."

"Do you know if Jennifer plans to attend?" he had to ask.

"Last I heard she did. She's very good at keeping her commitments."

"I would really like to get her opinion of the performance," Ed replied as the elevator stopped at the third floor.

"The children's ward is just down the hall. There are several cancer patients here. They all could use some uplifting entertainment. I really admire people like you, Ed."

"Thank, you, and I admire you, and others like you who work with these children trying to make their lives better. Our goals are identical," and he smiled at her.

They were at the entrance to the ward and Natalie said, "I'll introduce you as soon as we get inside."

When they entered the room he could see about thirty children in chairs, some in wheelchairs positioned in a semi-circle. Some of them had an IV apparatus next to them. Ed's appearance brought smiles to some of their faces, and a few of them exchanged words. They were all staring at him in his colorful costume.

"Children," Natalie began, "I want you to meet Laffy the clown. He is here to entertain you. Let's give him a big HELLO."

"HELLO LAFFY," they said in very loud unison.

"Hello, children," Ed greeted them. I'm very happy to be here to entertain you today," and as he looked around at the children, he suddenly noticed Abigail and Jennifer standing a few feet from each other in a corner of the room. It was a welcome sight, and he felt inspired.

"Now children, pay close attention to Laffy because he has quite an afternoon planned for you," and she gestured with her arm for him to take over.

Ed sat down on a chair and placed a small box on the floor. He raised his voice an octave higher and said, "Hi, are we ready to begin?" and as the words came from his large red lips he began to laugh. "I'm sorry, children, but I have a problem," said Ed. I just can't stop laughing," and he continued laughing and hopping around the room holding his stomach. Some of the children started laughing with him.

Ed glanced at Abigail, then at Jennifer. They both were smiling.

He turned his attention back to the children. "Oh my, perhaps you children can help me. If you laugh, then maybe I won't laugh as much. Do you think you can try to help me?" and he laughed even more.

Jennifer leaned toward Abigail and said softly, "Nice touch."

"I'm not surprised. He has his act together." He's one great guy," she said in adulation.

"Do you know him?" Jennifer asked.

"Yes, I do. We are going together," and she said it strongly.

"By the way, I'm Jennifer Sweet, Director of Public Relations here at the hospital," she said extending her hand.

"I'm Abigail, McCloud, and its nice meeting you, Jennifer," and she shook her hand. "I understand you interviewed Ed last week."

"Yes, I did. I can see he is very talented and cares a great deal about children. Very good qualities in a man, and I admire it."

"I feel very fortunate that he's all mine," said Abigail. After the comment, Jennifer returned her attention to the show.

"Why do you laugh so much?" a young girl was asking.

"I guess I was born jolly," and he laughed again. Then there was a muffled sound coming from the box on the floor. Still laughing, Ed bent down, and after opening the box pulled out a small dummy. The children looked on in silent amazement. It was an exact replica of Laffy the clown. Then, staring at the children, Laffy the dummy spoke. "He was born a nut." The comment brought a roar of laughter from the children.

"What's his name?" a boy with freckles asked.

"He is called Little Laffy, the miniature clown."

"He looks just like you," a younger patient said excitedly.

"You are correct, my friend."

"No, I don't," said the dummy. "He's ugly and I'm handsome," and the children were laughing again.

Abigail and Jennifer were laughing as much as the children. They were genuinely impressed with Ed's act.

"How can he be ugly if he looks just like you?" and the question was directed to the dummy by a girl leaning forward in her wheelchair.

"I'm going to pretend I didn't hear that," answered the dummy, and then added, "I still think he's a nut and the squirrels are looking for him." The children began to roar with laughter while clapping their hands.

"You had better be nice, Little Laffy, or I'll put you back in the box," threatened Ed.

"I'll be nice," the dummy quickly answered while softly mumbling, "He's still a nut." Then he quickly reached up and dislodged Ed's big red nose causing it to fall to the floor. The children reacted with a burst of loud screams and laughter.

Ed quickly glanced at Jennifer in the back of the room. She was laughing and holding one hand under her eye to stop the teardrops from running down her cheek.

"That was disrespectful, Little Laffy. Now you have to be punished. What do you think I should do with him children?"

"Spank him," said a young patient. Then another said, "Pull his nose off," and some of the girls screamed. The children now were totally into Ed's act, and Abigail and Jennifer were looking on bright eyed and cheerful.

"You heard the children, Little Laffy. Your nose must come off too," and when Ed tried to remove it, the dummy started moving away from him in different directions. The children were laughing and some were screaming, and one little girl wheeled her chair up to Ed and reached out with her hand as if to gesture a signal of peace.

"Wait," she said. "Give him a chance to apologize. If he doesn't, then take his nose off."

"You're quite the diplomat," Ed said to her, totally impressed. Some of the children were shouting take it off and others were saying no.

"All right, children," said Ed. "Tell you what. Since we appear to be divided, how about trying another approach? What if we give him the chance to pick up my nose and stick it back on after he says he's very sorry? All in favor raise your hands," and his eyes scanned the group of children. Better than half raised their hands.

"Okay, the vote is in favor of giving Little Laffy a chance to redeem himself. Thank the children, Little Laffy."

"I don't want to," and the dummy placed his face on Ed's shoulder.

Ed quickly took hold of his head and turned it to face the children. "Thank the children, Little Laffy, and don't be rude."

"I don't want to," Little Laffy repeated causing more laughter.

"Okay, I have had enough. I'm getting the box."

"Please don't get the box. I'll thank them," and he moved his mouth but did not speak.

"What kind of a thank you is that?" asked Ed frowning.

"A silent one, you nut," and there was another outburst of laughter.

And in the back of the room Jennifer was laughing so hard she was holding her stomach, and Abigail's eyes were tearing.

"Okay, I've had enough. You're going into the box," and Ed grabbed hold of the box on the floor next to him.

"No, No," Little Laffy pleaded.

"Well then, thank the children."

"Okay," said Little Laffy, and he put his head down not looking at anyone.

"I'm waiting," said Ed.

Little Laffy suddenly lifted his head and quickly said, "Thank you, children."

"Did you hear that children? Was it loud enough?"

"I couldn't hear him," said one of the children in the second row.

"Okay Little Laffy, you better say thank you again, and really mean it this time."

Little Laffy stood up and shouted, "Thank you, children," and immediately sat down on Ed's lap prompting more laughter.

"Thank you, Little Laffy. See, that wasn't so difficult, was it?" said Ed.

Little Laffy nodded yes, getting more laughter.

"Now let's get serious. Pick up my nose and place it back on my face. Do you think you can do that?"

Little Laffy nodded yes. Ed then manipulated his dummy so that he had the nose in his hand. "Now, please stick my nose back on my face," Ed commanded.

Little Laffy turned and looked at the children, then quickly placed the nose on Ed's forehead, arousing laughter from the children.

"What are you doing? That's not where my nose should be. Please put it where it belongs," he said annoyed with Little Laffy's behavior.

Little Laffy took the nose and promptly stuck it between Ed's eyes, and the room was roaring with laughter. Jennifer was pumping her hand with her thumb up conveying her kudos to Ed.

"Last chance to do it right, or it's in the box you go wise guy," said Ed.

"I won't do it," said Little Laffy, and Ed took hold of the box and immediately placed Laffy in it slamming the cover shut.

The younger children moaned and the older children laughed when they heard Little Laffy pleading to be let out.

"Okay, Little Laffy," said Ed. "I'll make a deal with you. If you thank the children for letting us come and visit with them today, and if you shake hands with them, I'll let you out of the box. Is it a deal?"

"Okay, I'll do it."

"Scouts honor?"

"Scouts honor," Little Laffy promised.

Ed removed him from the box so he could address the children. "Thank you, children for letting us visit today."

"Will you come visit us again?" asked the little girl who had wheeled her chair up to Ed.

"We'd love to," answered Ed, initiating cheering and clapping from the children.

Natalie West then walked over and stood by Ed's side raising her arm requesting silence. When the noise quieted down she spoke. "In behalf of the hospital staff and the children, I want to thank you, Mr. McDowell, for visiting us and putting on a splendid show. Now children, let's show Mr. McDowell and his little partner how much we appreciate his visit by giving him a round of applause," and everyone clapped loudly.

When the clapping came to an end, Ed walked closer to the children. "Before Little Laffy greets every one of you, I want to remind you to be certain to make laughter a part of your life every day. Laughter is contagious, my dear children, and it has a medicinal affect on your body. To put it simply, it nourishes your body like food and oxygen. Remember, every time you laugh you will be making someone else laugh too because laughter is what?"

"Contagious," responded the children.

"And now," said Ed, "my partner wants to shake hands with every one of you wonderful children."

After Ed had circulated his dummy among the children, Abigail and Jennifer joined him.

"You were fantastic, Ed," said Jennifer. You certainly have a way with children. You definitely have to appear again."

"That could be a problem," said Abigail. "I really don't like sharing him," and she took hold of his arm. Abigail's comment took Ed by surprise. Is she serious, or just joking, he thought.

"I'm sorry to hear that. The children will be so disappointed," Jennifer said as she looked at Ed for support.

"I'm sure we can get together again, Jennifer. It would be my pleasure to entertain the children again."

"Thanks again, Ed," said Jennifer shaking his hand. "Natalie will show you out," and she headed back to her office.

When Ed and Abigail left the hospital on the way to the parking lot, Abigail said, "That woman is hot on you. It's so damn obvious. I saw the way she looked at you."

"Whoa, whoa, now," said Ed. Take it easy. You're kidding, right?"

"No, I'm not," and she wasn't.

"And how can you tell, if I may ask?" trying to make light of her comment.

"My female intuition, my dear; She can be trouble," Abigail continued.

"Only if you let her, and do I detect some jealousy here?" and he smiled at her.

"Maybe some," she confessed.

"I'm flattered. Anyway, you have nothing to worry about. I have my hands full with you. I don't need another woman in my life," and he placed his arm around her waist.

"You better mean that. Now, give me a kiss," and he kissed her, construing her comment as another manifestation of her deepening feelings for him.

As they approached the parking lot Ed said, "Where did you park, Abigail?"

"In that area," she said pointing.

"That's good, and I'm just a little way past you." When they approached her car, something didn't seem right. Then Ed saw it first. "You have two flat tires on this side of your car."

"Oh, my God!" said Abigail with distress. "How could that happen?"

He walked over to the other side of the car. "I was afraid I would see this. These are flat also," he hated telling her.

"I don't believe this. Somebody had to do this. You don't just get four flat tires. Who the hell would want to do this to me?" she tried to reason.

Upon further examination, Ed noticed the tires had been slashed. "It was done deliberately Abigail. They were slashed."

"Son-of-a-bitch," she blurted, unable to control herself. She started pacing, venting her frustration. "I can't believe this. I just can't," she lamented.

Ed walked over and placed his hand on her shoulder. "I know you're upset, but maybe we can deduce some reason or conclusion about this," and he gave her a hug. "First, there is always the possibility someone was out for kicks and selected your car at random. With all the cars parked around here, the odds for that to happen would not be in your favor. So I suspect someone singled your car out."

"Great," she cried. That makes me feel good. What will they try next?" The mere thought made her anxious.

Ed studied her for a moment. Then he said, "Can you think of anyone who might be angry or upset with you? What about a shunned suitor?" he said grouping for any information that might be helpful.

She looked into the distance for a moment, thinking, and then shook her head saying, "No, I can't think of anyone."

Ed squatted and examined the front tire again noticing two slits, and he quickly checked out the remaining three.

She watched him moving abut like a sleuth, wondering what he was doing. "They are all the same. They all have two slits," he informed her.

She appeared calmer now. "What does that mean?" she asked.

"It could mean the individual is an organized person, exact or precise in what he or she does."

"I find that most interesting, Ed. Do you have training for this kind of thing?"

"No, no training, just common sense and keen observation. In the military, I was involved in a couple of mystery productions and I picked up a few pointers here and there."

"I'm impressed."

He smiled at her. Then he became serious, his eyes not moving, giving every indication he was deep in thought.

"What are you thinking?" she asked, her curiosity aroused.

"The phone calls, Abigail. There were two, only two. I think there is a connection. In fact, I'm almost certain."

"My, God," and she became unnerved. They had been eerie calls, and she had hoped they were just pranks. "It's so ironical. A little while ago we had some good laughs, and now we have what could be a serious problem. I don't like this, Ed," and he could see she was frightened.

"It's going to be okay," he tried to assure her. "Right now we have to get your car towed so you can get some new tires."

"How can they tow it with flats," she said frowning.

"They'll use a flat bed. It's quite an apparatus."

"I guess I can't think straight. Of course, they have all kinds of equipment. I just want to get this over with," her voice anxious.

"Don't worry, Abigail. I'll take care of it."

"Thanks, Ed. I feel more secure with you here. You're such a good friend, and I know you'll protect me," and she gave him a strong hug.

Of course he would protect her. He was truly concerned someone might try to harm her.

But he couldn't help think about the protection paradox that confronted him. How could he protect her from Conrad's plan to deliver a destructive blow to her heart when he was to be the implementer?

CHAPTER 9

"I'll pick you up at noon, Ed," Conrad was saying. "There's a vendor who sells great dogs at County Park, and I thought we could grab a bite to eat and get some fresh air while you fill me in on the latest developments between you and Abigail," he continued expecting Ed's total cooperation.

"Sure, Conrad, I'll be ready." He would always be ready, even if he didn't want to. The commander-in-chief was calling the shots. He wasn't dealing with some non commissioned officer or some other high-ranking military official. He had made a commitment with the man at the top, and that's how it had to be.

Conrad was punctual, and he was at the condo to pick Ed up at noon. As anxious as he was to be informed of the latest developments, he refrained from asking Ed anything concerning him and Abigail. He would wait until they were at the park.

When they arrived at the park, Conrad bought two hotdogs and two sodas and gave Ed one of each. "If you don't like the dog, Ed, its tough shit," and he smiled wryly.

After taking a bite, Ed said, "Great dog, Conrad."

"I like your spirit of cooperation, Ed. Cooperation is such a good thing, so much better than compromise. Compromise can so easily lead to defeat. Did you know that, Ed?"

"I guess I haven't given it much thought. Should I?" he asked looking straight ahead.

"Let's say it behooves you," and Conrad said no more.

They walked in silence while eating. When they were finished, Conrad was the first to speak. "Let's go sit on a bench by the pond," he said pointing. A large tree shaded the bench, and a short distance away a mother and her two children were feeding a group of ducks in the water.

Once seated, Conrad looked at Ed and said, "So tell me, how is your relationship with Abigail going?"

"It's going good, Conrad. Our relationship is going in the right direction. I do believe she cares about me," and he was hoping he wouldn't have to go into specific details.

"And what do you have to back that statement up?" It appeared that Conrad wanted specific details.

"Well, she did mention the L word once."

"The L word," Conrad quickly replied. "You mean love?"

"Yes, she said it once. Just once," he quickly added.

"And what brought that about, sex?"

"No, no, it wasn't that." He didn't like lying, but he felt uncomfortable discussing the content of his sexual encounters with Abigail. The mere fact that Conrad had fallen in love with her and had spent the last year in a relationship that obviously included a lot of sexual activity, contributed to his on going reluctance to discuss the subject.

"I gave her a giraffe when I went over for dinner. She was so pleased she said I love you."

Conrad looked at him long, as if trying to reach his mind through his eyes. "I'm surprised she didn't want to give you her body as a gesture of appreciation."

"She did hint about having sex, but I discouraged her," and somehow he felt Conrad didn't believe him. He knew Conrad wasn't a fool, and that he soon would have to let him know that he had had sex with Abigail.

He also had noticed a change in Conrad's behavior towards him ever since he had agreed to court Abigail. He appeared to be more distant and quizzical. Conrad's attitude even went to the extent of making Ed feel he doubted the validity of some of his statements concerning Abigail. Unfortunately, he didn't expect any change in Conrad's behavior.

"How much longer do you think it's going to take to get her totally involved with you?" Conrad asked.

"It's hard to say, buddy. I entertained the children at the hospital the other day and Abigail attended the show. The children had a great time and it touched her. I guess she looked at me as some kind of hero of compassion. I believe it intensified her feelings for me."

Conrad studied Ed for a moment. "That's good, Ed. That's very good. And if you make love to her it should be the icing on the cake," and he smiled.

"I'll definitely work on it," and he wondered why Conrad was so preoccupied with sex.

"I know you can do this, Ed. Put the witch up there," he said raising his hand, "then drop her hard. That's the moment I'm waiting for," and his eyes seemed to come to life. "I know I'm redundant about this, but she has to pay. You do understand?" he said trying to reaffirm his commitment.

"Yes, I do, buddy," and he made a mental note of Conrad referring to Abigail for the first time as a witch and not a bitch.

Conrad stared for a moment at the mother with her children feeding the ducks across from them, and said to Ed, "She sure has a nice ass. Speaking about ass, this bench is starting to get to mine," and he stood up. "I'm out of here, Ed. I have some things to do. Next time you can buy the dogs."

Erica Hollis was putting on the finishing touches to her makeup. Conrad would be picking her up in fifteen minutes. He had taken her up on her offer to get together. When he had called she had suggested they have a picnic lunch at the beach. It hadn't taken her long during their phone conversation to express a love of the ocean. Even though he could take it or leave it, he had quickly agreed to the picnic lunch. To him, it had been a strategic move to let her decide what they should do during their initial time together. It was the commencement of his calculating plan to form a bonding relationship with the beauty queen. The plan was simple. Please her.

When he pulled into the driveway of the Hollis residence, he was impressed with the house. It was a large two story English Tudor, which visibly conveyed wealth. He had no previous knowledge of Erica's family background, and as far as personal information went he knew she was intelligent and energetic.

It was Erica who greeted him at the door. "Hi, Conrad, my folks aren't home. So unfortunately, you don't get to meet them, and I'm disappointed they can't meet you."

"Then there will have to be a next time."

"That sounds good, my dear. The picnic basket is in the kitchen. I'll get it and then we can leave," and his eyes followed her until she turned into the kitchen. Physically, she was stunning in her white shorts and yellow halter that exposed her midsection.

When she returned, she was smiling and her eyes reflected enthusiasm. "You get to taste my chicken."

"I can't wait. If it's as good as you look, it will be just great," and there would be more compliments.

"I'm sure you won't be disappointed," and her confidence couldn't be more evident.

When they were outside Erica said, "Its good convertible weather. If you don't object, I'll take my mom's car."

"Not at all," he said as he continued to honor her choices.

"In thirty minutes Erica had them at a private beach, and it was evident to Conrad that she had a heavy foot when she drove. She parked the car twenty-five feet away from the shoulder inland toward the beach.

"My uncle Seth owns property here, so I have my own, little private section of beach," she said as she removed her clothing revealing a flimsy, red bikini. "I hope you have a bathing suit under your trousers," expecting him to say yes as she raised the picnic basket out of the car.

"I do," and he removed his clothing, exposing blue trunks.

"Looking pretty sexy," she teased him raising her eyebrows.

"You're the epitome of sex in that bathing suit, Erica," and he returned the compliment meaning every word.

"If you saw my younger sister Debbie, you would be saying that to her instead of me.

"You mean there is someone out there that has you beat?"

"I'm afraid so. It's a non-classic case of sibling rivalry, due to the fact my sister and I get along just fine. We're really supportive of each other," and she said it with sincerity.

"I'll never have to worry about sibling rivalry. I'm an only child, and I'm sure I was an accident," he said looking down at the sand.

Erica studied him for a moment. "Hey, do I see pouting? None of that today," and she placed her hand on his shoulder. "Perhaps some time in your life you will have the opportunity to bring wanted children into the world. I hope to have three or more someday," and she smiled at him.

"I would want two," he said. "Just two," he repeated.

"That's a good number for a small family. One of each sex would be nice." Then she changed the subject. "What do you say we eat and get caught up on old times?"

"Sure, Erica," he again agreed. "My stomach would welcome some food about now." He was hungry, and knowing her lunch contained chicken only enhanced his appetite.

They spread a large blanket on the sand, and sat down. Erica immediately opened the picnic basket. In it there was chicken, bread, potato salad and wine.

"Everything looks so good, Erica. I'll start with a piece of chicken, thank you." After a few bites he said, "Excellent taste. You must be good in the kitchen."

"I'm good at whatever I do. That's not conceit it's confidence," she quickly added.

"No question in my mind about it," he agreed.

"So what do you want out of life?" he asked.

"My primary goal is to find a man that will love me and give me the children that I want. I want to be a loving mom. I also like working with the public."

She definitely had the personality for it. And she was a compassionate, giving woman who genuinely loved children. She had a good relationship with her parents and sister over the years, and though she had her own apartment, she still saw her family often. It was easy to see that her very being was anchored to a deep set of family roots.

He digested what she said and then asked, "How serious are you about competing in pageants? Doesn't it make demands on your time?"

"It does make demands, but I enjoy it. More importantly, my life circumstances right now are such that I have plenty of time for it."

He stared at her blue-green eyes for a moment. "In other words, if you had a blooming, romantic relationship with someone you might be diverted away from pageants?" and he waited for her response.

"I'd say that is a good interpretation."

He was hoping she would say that, and he picked up the bottle of wine and filled her glass, then his. "I'm still puzzled why a girl of your beauty and charm is still unattached." I hope I'm not stepping out of bounds."

"Not at all, Conrad," she said. If you remember, I told you I had an unsuccessful marriage. It was a mistake, and this time around I'm being much more selective and careful."

"Good for you. There are a lot of creeps out there. I mean for both sexes," he was quick to clarify. "You know, Erica," and he paused to sip some wine, "When we were in school my circle of friends referred to you as the penis erector. That's the effect your presence had. You should take it as a compliment."

"Oh, my God!" she said laughing hard. "I wish I knew then. Did I really make that happen?" and the conversation made her glance at his crouch causing them both to laugh.

"If I may continue with the frankness of this conversation, Mr. Morgan, the science teacher, always stared at your ass when you walked out of his classroom. I think he was a pervert," said Conrad making her laugh.

"You're full of information. And you're sure of these things?"

"Absolutely," he insisted.

"Gee, I didn't know I had that kind of affect on boys," and he believed that she probably hadn't. "I have to make a confession. Remember when you came to the dealership I said I had a crush on you in school? Well, I referred to you as doll face to my friends. But that wasn't all. We use to fantasize how you would be in bed," and she was comfortable talking about it.

Her true confession made him laugh. "Perhaps I can make your fantasy a reality."

"I'll keep that in mind. So, what have you done since you graduated high school?" Erica asked.

"I spent three years in military service, and then two years in college studying engineering. The hitch in the military was for me. As for college, that was for my father. His dream is to have me take over his business when he's ready to hand it over. In the interim, he wants me to work with him," and he paused helping himself to some potato salad.

"That sounds like a promising and financially secure future, Conrad."

"I see it as a parental, controlled environment. I feel my actions will always be under scrutiny. I don't know how long I'll be able to cope with it," and that's all he planned to tell her. She must not know that he was recently jilted by Abigail and on the rebound, or that he hadn't worked in almost two months. She had to think he had a genuine interest in her and that he obviously was interested in pursuing a meaningful relationship.

"I hope it works out for you. You should definitely enjoy your work." She studied him for a moment, moistening her lips. "Do you mind if I ask if you have had any close relationships since we were in school?" And she really wanted to know.

He had a suspicion she would ask that question. After all, they were being candid with each other. He would answer her, working around Abigail. "Yes, I have, but not recently."

"How did you manage to stay single?" She was anxious to hear his answer.

"Perseverance," he answered, "and it wasn't easy."

She looked at him quizzically. "So, if I understand you correctly, you're saying you didn't allow any of the girls in the past to capture your heart?"

He hesitated a moment before answering her. "I guess I wasn't totally convinced I had found the right girl for me."

"Nothing is certain in life, Conrad. But we can't let uncertainty and doubt hold us back. Otherwise, we would live dull, uneventful lives," and she felt a sense of loss for him.

Oh, he knew about uncertainty. More than she could ever imagine. And he knew all to well about vulnerability and irreparable pain. It made him wonder how much pain she had endured in her life.

"It's all water over the dam," he said. "Everything we do is experience and stored memory. So, all is not lost. My attitude is subject to change with the right persuasion," and he smiled at her.

He raised his wine glass and drank from it until it was empty. "Erica, I think we could use a good laugh. Remember Porky Lewis?"

"Yes, I do. How could I forget, when he almost knocked me over when we were in the school cafeteria. God forbid if you got in his way in the food line."

"I know what you mean. He was in my physical Ed class after lunch. Some of us guys would take hold of him and press his stomach. He would burp and fart at the same time. We gave him the nickname, the Stereo Kid," and it made Erica burst out in laughter.

"How creative of you guys," she said. That's a riot. It would be great for a comedy show," and he agreed sharing her laughter.

"Let's go in the water, and when we come out we can build a sand castle," Conrad suggested.

"Race you to the water," she said as she started for the ocean. He let her reach the water first. "You're pretty fast," he praised her.

"I do everything well, remember?" and he wondered what she would be like in bed.

They frolicked in the water, reminiscent of their high school days. He carried her on his shoulders and spilled her into the water. They did several handstands and mimicked whales. When they had had enough, he carried her out of the water and dropped her on the sand.

"That was great, Conrad," her face beaming with enjoyment. "I haven't had so much fun in a long time. Thank, you," and she kissed him softly on the cheek.

"I enjoyed myself too. Are you in the mood to build a castle?" Conrad asked.

"Sure. How about right here?" and she sat where the sand was moist, a little distance away from the foam of the incoming waves.

"Can I be the architect?" she asked.

"Why not, you do everything well," he teased.

She quickly made a sketch in the sand with her finger. "Do you approve?"

He studied it for a moment. "I think you should only have two large towers. It bothers me to have more."

"It does, does it? What are you going to do, knock them down if I don't do as you say?"

"No, I'm going to knock you down," and he wrestled her to the ground making her laugh. When she stopped laughing, she looked into his eyes. He stared back, slowly moving his lips toward hers. In a fraction he was kissing her long and gently. Then he lifted himself from the ground and said, "Come on, let's build that castle."

During the ride back to Erica's home, they chose to listen to a disk that featured relaxing sounds of nature. It added to the rich fulfillment of the day.

After Erica parked the car in the driveway she said, "I had a great day, Conrad. Thanks again."

"The pleasure was mine. Will I see you again?" he asked.

"Absolutely," and it was the answer he wanted to hear.

"You call me now," she called out as he got into his car, and as he drove away he blew her a kiss.

Later that evening, Conrad reviewed the events of the day in his mind. No question she had had a great time. She had thanked him twice. What better proof could he ask for? He was certain he had rekindled her high school crush on him. He could only construe his efforts of the day were successful toward achieving his goal. How could he grade himself with anything less than an A plus, and ironically, he had had a good time himself. He felt uneasy as he realized that he could actually like her, but his being was consumed with a relentless vengeance for Abigail and the female gender, and unfortunately, it also made Erica a target to be brought down too.

CHAPTER 10

It was Saturday morning, and the sky was filled with layers of dark clouds that blotted out the sun. The forecast called for showers for the duration of the day.

Abigail McCloud disliked gloomy rain days. She would be spending the morning at the McPherson Point Convalescent Home as a volunteer, and it offered some consolation from the weather outside. As she drove to the convalescent home, her mind was preoccupied with Ed and when she would be seeing him later in the evening. It would be the first time they would be going out with another couple, her friend, Barbara Willis and her fiancé, Roy. Yes, she had been so preoccupied she didn't notice the black vehicle that followed her from her apartment.

After she parked and got out of her car, she raised and opened a pink umbrella and walked briskly to the main entrance. Inside she was greeted at the desk. "Good Morning, Abigail."

"Hi, Jean, how are you this gloomy morning?" and the tone of her voice was cheerful.

"As good as I'll ever be," and she placed her hand on her arthritic hip. "The rain gets to me," and she rolled her eyes.

"Hang in there, lady," Abigail said encouragingly.

"Sure, by the hip until dead," and the comment made Abigail laugh. "Where do I start this morning?"

"In "A" wing, my dear," Jean informed her. And Abigail, Mr. Roberts is hallucinating again about his dog Skip. I just thought I'd warn you."

"Sure, no problem, Jean," said Abigail. She enjoyed working with the elderly. She wanted so much to make them feel loved and important. She alternated weeks between the hospital and the convalescent home.

Her first stop was Mrs. Parsons, and Abigail greeted her with her customary, "How are you this morning?" and as usual, she didn't respond. It was nothing new. Mrs. Parsons was eighty-three years old and highly suspicious of people. That fact, coupled with her not being a morning person limited her conversation.

"Are you comfortable, Mrs. Parsons? Here, let me prop your pillow for you," and she followed Abigail's every movement with her eyes.

"I'm going to place this magazine by your bed in case you feel like reading later," said Abigail smiling warmly. "I'm going to leave you now, but I'll be back later, okay?"

"When she was almost out the door she heard Mrs. Parsons say, "Hi." Abigail smiled, shook her head and headed for the next room.

"Abigail wait," Jean called out to her. "You have an urgent phone call in the lobby."

"Did they say who it was?" she asked suddenly feeling nervous.

"They didn't say."

"I hope nothing is wrong," she said to herself as she picked up the phone. "Hello, this is Abigail." There was no response. "Hello, this is Abigail," she repeated. Then she heard the heavy breathing and the high-pitched wailing sound that made her drop the receiver onto the desk with a loud bang.

"Oh, my God!" she cried.

"What's wrong, dear?" Jean asked alarmed.

"Oh, my God," she repeated. "How do they know I'm here?" her face white from fear.

"What is it, Abigail? What is it?" Jean asked trying to get a clue as to what was wrong.

"I think someone is trying to harm me. That's all I can say."

"Do you want me to call security?"

"I don't know. Give me a moment to think," said a frightened Abigail, and she placed her hands on her temples. Last time there had been two phone calls before the tire-slashing incident, and some time had elapsed before the second call. She wouldn't panic. She would call Ed. Yes, she would call Ed. "No, Jean, don't call security. There is nothing they can do," and she appeared calmer.

"Are you sure, dear?"

"Yes, Jean, I'm sure. I decided to call my friend Ed." At first her nerves made her dial the number incorrectly. When she redialed, each ring of the phone seemed like an eternity. After the fifth ring she heard Ed say "Hello."

She was relieved when she heard his voice. "Ed, I'm so glad you are there," and he instantly knew she was distressed.

"What's wrong, Abigail?" he asked before she could speak another word.

"I had one of those wailing phone calls, here at the convalescent home. They said I had an urgent call, and when I answered, the breathing and wailing sound was there again," she rambled.

"Slow down, Abigail, and try to be calm," he tried to console her.

"Ed, how did they know I was here? This is so scary. I'm a wreck."

He knew it was an understatement. "I know you are. Try to be calm. Continue working and I'll come down."

"Thank you, Ed. I'd like that. You're such a good friend, and I feel better already," and she took a deep breath.

"Good girl. Eventually, I'll get my hands on the sorry bastard," and his words were forceful. "Don't leave the building for any reason," he cautioned her.

"Oh, I won't," she assured him.

After a hot cup of coffee, she continued with her rounds visiting the patients in "A" wing though her attention drifted from time to time to the faceless enemy that had emerged into her life.

While she worked she utilized every cell of her brain to try again to come up with an answer, as to who could have singled her out as a target for harassment, but it was to no avail. She hadn't a single clue as to who it was or why it was happening. It left her both fearful and frustrated. She clung to the hope that perhaps Ed could come up with something enlightening.

When she finished her rounds, Ed was waiting for her. "I'm so glad you're here," and she gave him a strong hug. His appearance alone reinforced her strength.

"We'll get to the bottom of this," he tried to comfort her. He also was certain another call would be coming soon.

She had been thinking the same thing. "You do know I'm going to get another call."

"I'm afraid you are, Abigail. The only uncertainty is when. I don't want to frighten you, but I think it's going to be soon," and he hated saying it. He wondered what the punishment would be this time. Would it be directed at her personally, or would it be at another one of her possessions?

She was ready to leave and Jean was concerned. "You be careful, my dear."

"I will. I have my bodyguard. He will take care of me," she said hoping it would ease Jean's worry.

"I'll follow you home, Abigail, and I'll be looking for anything suspicious."

When he followed her, he kept a reasonable distance behind trying not to be conspicuous in the event someone did have intentions of following her. He had seen nothing when they reached her apartment. He went in with her to make sure everything was okay and enhance her sense of security.

She knew he had to go to his condo to get ready for their date later. She looked at him adoringly. "I love you, Ed. I'm so grateful I met you. I owe that tire everything. Who would ever imagine a flat tire would bring two people together," and she walked up to him and gave him a hug resting her head against his chest.

He could imagine, and her words rang in his ears. For the first time he truly felt like a calculating conspirator.

She looked into his eyes, her arms still around him. "I don't want to let you go, but I know you have to get ready for our date and drive back here."

"I'll call you later to be sure everything is all right," he promised.

"I love you," she again told him.

"I love you too, Abigail," and he kissed her on the forehead.

"God, I love that guy," she said after she closed the door behind him.

When Ed walked into the condo, the phone was ringing. "Conrad, it has to be Conrad," he told himself. He had come to the conclusion that Conrad somehow possessed an uncanny ability to call him whenever he first stepped into the condo. He picked up the phone and said, "Yes, Conrad."

"Ed, this is Abigail. He just called. It's the second call. How quickly it came. Something awful is going to happen. It's going to be different this time. I can sense it," and she started to sob.

"That son-of-a-bitch," said Ed with anger. "The low life has frightened you again. He's going to be sorry he started this," and he was angry.

"I'm afraid, Ed. I'm really afraid this time," and she continued sobbing.

Whoever it was had finally made her cry, and obviously was wearing her down. It was the first time he had heard her cry, and it disturbed him emotionally. "Please don't cry, Abigail. You're safe in the house. I'll be over shortly. I'll take some clothes and shower at your place, and I'll stay with you tonight," and he hoped his words would quickly comfort her.

"Okay, but please hurry. I don't want to be alone. This whole thing makes me feel like a fly on the wall ready to be swatted."

"I'll be there before you know it. Take a few deep breaths and try to relax. I'm going to hang up now, and I'll be right there."

"Okay. Please hurry," she repeated, and he hung up the phone.

Ed was out of the condo in minutes. When he started driving, he suddenly realized what he had said when he answered the phone. "My, God!" he blurted. "I said yes, Conrad. Damn, she had to have heard it," he reasoned talking out loud. How could he have been so careless? When he thought of the possible consequences it made his heart race, and he could feel the blood flowing in his temples. She was already upset, and it definitely wasn't the time to hear the name Conrad. How could he have been so careless? He kept rehashing his dilemma through his mind as he drove, wondering what he would say if she questioned him. Then he tried to abate his anxiety by thinking of the possibility she hadn't heard him. She was upset when she had called, and perhaps oblivious to what he had said when he had first answered the phone. After all, she had never mentioned the name Conrad during their phone conversation. He chose to think of the latter possibility. He had to stay calm and convey to her an attitude of strength and determination, not one of fear and weakness. She was depending on him for courage and resolve.

When he arrived at her apartment, he could physically see the stress she was experiencing brought on by the last phone call. "Ed, I'm so glad you're here," and she gave him a long hug. "I've never hugged anyone as much as I've hugged you," and she smiled at him lovingly.

"That's good, just as long as you don't crack my ribs," he said jokingly.

"Not even one?" and he was pleased to see her return the humor.

He held her by her shoulders and said, "Smile now, we can't let Barbara and Roy see us looking scared and worried. I don't want them to think your boyfriend is some of kind of nerd."

"They could never think you're some kind of nerd. All I have to tell them is you're one hell of a sex machine," and she tried to keep a straight face, but couldn't and started to laugh.

"So that's it. You want me for my body."

"Of course I do. I'd have to be a fool not to want your beautiful body." Then smiling she added, "And all the other inner qualities you possess."

"Thank, you. You just redeemed yourself."

"And why do you love me?" and she looked at him with seductive eyes.

"For your body, of course," and he struggled to keep from laughing.

"Oh you… you're terrible," and she punched him in the shoulder. "I know why you do, and it's all for the right reasons. Plus this," and she turned and slapped herself on the butt.

"You're something else, Abigail," and he was pleased to see their engagement in some repartee temporarily made them forget about the psychopath who was harassing her.

They both showered, but the stress of the wailing phone calls along with the time constraint of her friends expected arrival eliminated any possibility of a complete, sexual encounter.

After some deliberation, Abigail chose a light, green dress gathered at the waist with a dark green rope belt, which definitely complimented her flawless body. Around her neck was a delicate, gold necklace, which matched her earrings, and her eye shadow was almost the exact shade of her dress. The pupils of her eyes reflected the color of her dress making them predominately green. She completed her outfit with a pair of light green, strapped dress shoe with slender, four-inch heels drawing attention to her long, shapely limbs.

Ed looked at her admiringly. "I've never seen you look so beautiful, Abigail," and it raised his consciousness of her physical elegance to another level.

"Thank you, my darling. I hope I never disappoint you."

"You won't," he said. No, she wouldn't, but he would disappoint her, and it made him feel guilty. Terribly guilty, and for a moment he didn't like himself. He sat quietly for a moment reflecting on what he was doing, his eyes locked in one position staring straight ahead.

His concentration was broken when Abigail said, "Are you all right, my darling? You look spacey."

He hesitated. "Yes, of course. I'm fine," and he smiled at her.

"I forgot to tell you. Roy Bellows is Australian and has an English accent. I love to hear him speak."

"Really," Ed said somewhat surprised. Perhaps I should let him do most of the talking tonight and rest my vocal cords. A ventriloquist has to rest now and then," and he placed his hand on his throat and grimaced.

"Fine, as long as you don't rest something else," and she chuckled with her remark.

"I couldn't even if I wanted to."

"Are you trying to say I'm overactive?" and she walked up to him and took hold of his hands. "Well, I didn't hear an answer."

"You're insatiable, Abigail."

"And you love it," she said before he could say anything more. She started tickling him making him laugh. "Come on, say you're sorry, Ed," and she continued tickling him. "Okay, I'm sorry. Now you know my weakness."

"Now, I have a defense if you try to bully me, but I know I need not ever worry about you bullying or hurting me," and she kissed him looking straight into his eyes.

CHAPTER 11

Later in the evening, Barbara Willis and Roy Bellows arrived. Barbara was exactly five feet tall with red hair and green eyes, and was slightly overweight. She worked at the hospital as an x-ray technician where she had met Abigail. They immediately had developed a friendship and had become close friends.

Barbara's fiancé, Roy Bellows worked as a salesman and was employed by a large, pharmaceutical company. His position involved a good amount of travel, a condition he and Barbara had to reconcile themselves to out of necessity. Roy was tall, standing over six feet, with blonde hair and blue eyes. His complexion gave the appearance that his skin had never been exposed to the sun for any length of time.

"Since we're driving the SUV, why don't we go in our car," said Barbara.

"Yes, indeed," Roy agreed.

"We accept. Besides, it will give Ed and me a chance to make out before we get there," said Abigail expecting to get a rise out of everyone, particularly Ed.

Ed's cheeks became flushed. "Abigail, your friends just met me. You're going to give them a bad impression of me."

"We know she is a nut, Ed. And very sex oriented. If everyone was like her, the United States would be over populated," and Barbara looked at her with raised eyebrows.

"You're just jealous of my extraordinary libido," and Abigail raised her arms and swerved her hips making everyone laugh.

"See, I said she was a nut," and Barbara gave her friend a poke. It pleased Ed to see Abigail more relaxed and enjoying herself, and not focused on the events that had materialized earlier in the day.

"Are we ready to leave?" asked Barbara. She was a strong, willed girl with a domineering personality, and she felt extremely comfortable being in charge. "What's this place we're going to again?" and the question was directed to Abigail.

"It's a restaurant by the ocean next to a lighthouse. The old ships used the lighthouse for navigational purposes. One side of the dining room is high on a cliff that overlooks the ocean. It's really romantic when the moon is full," said Abigail as she took hold of Ed's arm.

"I should have known it would be romantic."

"Of course, Barbara," said Abigail. "What else is there? I bet Roy would like the place," and she looked at Roy for vindication.

"Yes, indeed." His level of sexual and romantic appetite far exceeded his fiancé's.

"I'm glad he travels a lot," said Barbara. "If he was around you a great deal he would become a sex, craving monster that would never leave me alone."

"You mean sex starved," Abigail teased her.

"Let's drop the sex for now and focus on food," said Ed who was predominately listening and enjoying the conversation.

"Yes, indeed," Roy commented laughing. "I could eat a bloody horse."

When they entered the vehicle, Ed could smell the newness of it.

"How long have you had your SUV, Roy?"

"One month today. First SUV I've owned. I think I'm sold on them. Yes, indeed."

Roy started the engine and turned half way around in the seat and said, "Where to, mates?"

"Abigail is the co-pilot. She's the only one who knows where the hell to go," said Barbara who disliked not being previously briefed regarding Abigail's mysterious choice.

Abigail gave Roy the first set of directions, and when he arrived at a four-way junction, she instructed him to take route 19. It was a lightly traveled, one lane road in a wooded area. Dark clouds had rolled in while they were approaching the intersection, blotting out the remaining daylight of the settling sun. The dark clouds were now dropping precipitation as they turned onto route 19.

A moment later, a vehicle was behind them with almost blinding, high beam lights. The vehicle then moved to within a foot of the back bumper of Roy's SUV.

"What's the bloody fool doing?" Roy blurted causing Barbara and Abigail to halt their conversation.

"What are you talking about?" Barbara asked.

"The bloody car behind us," and everyone turned and looked behind. The vehicle's high beams flashed off and on several times and then dropped back to within two car lengths.

"It looks like a pickup truck," said Ed.

"If he wants to pass, why doesn't he?" Roy assumed after seeing the lights flash off and on. His eyes were moving back and forth from the road to the rear view mirror. "He's moving up again," Roy informed them, and the vehicle was inches from their bumper.

A frightened Abigail looked at Ed. "It's him. I know it's him."

"Please stay calm, Abigail. We can't be sure," Ed replied as he tried to squelch any possibility of panic.

Barbara became alarmed after hearing the conversation between Ed and Abigail. "Did I hear you correctly, Abigail? You know who's behind us?" her voice full of concern.

"No, she doesn't," Ed answered. "She was just speculating."

"I want her to tell me," Barbara insisted.

"He's coming up fast," Roy's voice suddenly rang out. The pickup had dropped back, but now was approaching rapidly.

"The bloody fool is going to hit us," Roy warned, and his voice was strained. The pickup hit the rear bumper hard, making them jerk in their seats.

"That bastard," cried Barbara. "What does he want?"

Roy quickly accelerated, momentarily making the SUV move a distance ahead of the pickup. "Maybe I can outrun him," he thought out loud, his eyes looking in the rear view mirror.

Abigail turned to look at the pickup, her eyes squinting from the bright headlights. Again it was rapidly approaching giving her a feeling of dread. It hit hard a second time.

"The bloody bastard," shouted Roy in anger.

"Pull off the road," Barbara screamed, her fear heightened.

"No," Abigail pleaded. "They may have a gun. We can't stop. We must keep moving."

"I think they want to frighten us, and that's all," said Ed. "I don't think they want to get seriously involved with anything," and he hoped to be persuasive.

"The son-of-a-bitch is doing a good job of rattling us," said Barbara.

"Does anyone have a cell phone?" Abigail asked. "We can call 911 and get police assistance."

"I do," Barbara quickly answered. "Why the hell didn't anyone else think of it," and she looked in her purse. "Shit, I left the phone home. I was charging the freaking battery."

"Okay, anyone else have one?" Abigail asked again. No one came forward with a yes. She had left hers home because she wanted an evening out with no interruptions, a decision she now regretted. Knowing there could be no help heightened her fear.

"He's dropping back again," Roy announced. "The bloody fool appears to be staying back for now."

"I hope he's had enough. I've already lost my appetite," said Abigail.

"Wait a bloody minute. He's moving out. I think he's going to pass us," and the news sparked encouragement.

Ed looked over his shoulder to see the position of the pickup. It suddenly was almost next to the SUV. "Be ready, Roy. Whoever they are might try something," Ed cautioned.

"Indeed I'm ready."

When the pickup was beside them, Roy looked out his window and quickly tried to discern the driver. His view was obscured by the darkness and the beaded water drops on the window. "I can't see who's driving the bloody truck," Roy moaned.

Ed decided he would give it a try, and he leaned forward and looked into the cab. The same conditions prevented him from seeing anything definitive.

"Can you see anything?" Abigail asked hoping for any kind of a clue.

"I can't see anything," and he was visibly frustrated.

The pickup was half way past them when it suddenly veered to the right and slammed into the side of the SUV. The impact caused it to swerve to the right and then back and forth before Roy brought it under control.

"Oh, my God," Abigail cried placing her hands on the sides of her head.

"The crazy, bloody fool," Roy shouted. "I believe he's trying to injure us," and his anger quickly turned into fear.

"The sick bastard is also doing a job on our vehicle," cried Barbara. "I can imagine what it must look like."

"If he tries it again, Roy, don't try to hit him back. Maybe he'll become discouraged if we don't engage in combat with him," Ed tried to reason.

The pickup again was next to the SUV. Then it suddenly veered for a second hit, but Roy was able to turn away, reducing the impact.

Abigail cringed with the sound of the crash. "I can't take much more of this," she wailed.

"Pull off the road and stop," Ed quickly commanded. "I don't think whom ever they are will confront us."

Roy turned and looked at him, uncertain. "Do it, Roy. Let's chance it."

"Okay, mate," and he turned the SUV onto the shoulder and slowly brought it to a stand still. After passing them, the pickup slowed down momentarily, and then it accelerated. They watched it until the taillights disappeared into the darkness.

"That son-of-a-bitch almost made me wet my pants," said Barbara.

Roy got out and looked at the side of his SUV. "That bloody bastard wrecked the whole side," and his fear turned back into anger.

"Thank God none of us are hurt," said Abigail. "And you do have insurance, Roy?"

"Yes, I do. And the bloody fool is going to make my insurance go up. Can you imagine that," and he shrugged with grief.

"I still can't figure what this was all about," and Barbara stared into Abigail's eyes. "Do you know, Abigail?"

She had asked before, but for some reason Ed had dismissed her. Now Abigail would tell her the truth.

"I have a good idea why it happened," she confessed.

"Tell me, I'm all ears." Barbara's facial expression was stern and her lips were tight.

"A couple of weeks ago I received a horrible phone call. First there was heavy breathing, and then it was followed by a high-pitched wailing sound. A short time later I received another call. It was just like the first. I didn't know what to make of it. All I know is it gave me the creeps and I was frightened. I told Ed about it and he thought it could be some prank playing games with me."

Barbara was listening attentively, her face still stern. Roy and Ed were leaning against the SUV, Roy with his arms crossed. Abigail continued, "We took the situation more seriously after we discovered my car with four slashed tires in the parking lot where I do volunteer work. Each tire had two slits, and there were two phone calls. We assumed they were related." She paused to moisten her lips and swallow. "A couple of days ago the calls started again, the second one coming this morning."

"This morning," blurted Barbara. "It was the same scenario, and you were suspecting something to happen again. For Christ sake,

Abigail, you put Roy and me at risk," and her face was flushed with anger. "I'm appalled you could be that inconsiderate. No, I'm pissed and appalled."

"Barbara, please don't be angry. We didn't think they would target anyone but me."

"Well, you were wrong. You could have killed all of us. It would have been no different than you putting a gun to our heads and pulling the trigger," Barbara's eyes still reflecting anger.

"Barbara please, you're being over dramatic. And to put it in your words, I didn't pull the trigger after all," and Abigail was becoming annoyed. Barbara was treating her as if she was uncaring and insensitive. She had been frightened too.

"Do you realize that damn pickup truck could have made us roll over and spew our body parts all over the road," and Barbara wouldn't let go of the incident and criticism of Abigail.

"Let it go, Barbara. You're getting on my damn nerves." And with that said, Roy walked up to Barbara and took hold of her hand. "It's okay now. We're all friends. Don't say something you will regret later."

"Shut up, Roy," his words falling on her deaf ears.

"She's just being a bitch, Roy," said Abigail.

"I'm a bitch?" and Barbara's anger made her heart race. "I don't think so. Your head is screwed on wrong, honey. As a matter of fact, you're speaking through your ass, bitch."

Barbara's words infuriated Abigail, and she came charging at her. In an instant she had a hand full of Barbara's hair and was pulling on it relentlessly. Barbara wailed in pain before Ed was able to separate them.

"Enough," he shouted. "I can't believe you girls have let a faceless coward come between you. You're friends, for God sake. Doesn't that mean anything?"

They both looked at Ed, and then each other. Barbara rubbed her head where a cluster of her hair had been uprooted and gave Abigail a mean stare.

"I think you girls should apologize to each other and get over what has happened here tonight. Yes, indeed," said Roy.

"I can't do that, Roy. Not tonight. I just want to go home now," and Barbara left and seated herself in the SUV.

"She's being a stubborn bitch," said Abigail shaking her head in disbelief. "She doesn't have the right to be more upset than anyone of us."

"I guess the bloody incident rattled her nerves a great deal. I'm sorry for her actions," Roy apologized.

"Sure, and thanks for trying to make me feel better, Roy. I'd appreciate it if you could take us home now. Maybe I'll even get drunk."

Ed had never seen her so angry. She did have a temper, but in his opinion, Barbara did come on strong. Her words definitely had a cutting edge, and in Abigail's defense she had no way of knowing they would be attacked at that particular time.

The atmosphere in the SUV was sullen from a friendship gone sour, and the drive back to Abigail's apartment was void of conversation with the exception of Roy, on occasion, asking for directions. To Ed, it had been like riding in a hearse with a corpse unable to carry on a conversation. During the trip he had looked upon the girls as being reminiscent of a loaded shotgun ready to be triggered with the slightest comment between the two.

After Roy had dropped them off at Abigail's apartment, she seemed relieved to be home with Ed. As angry as she had been, she still had made a gesture toward reconciliation when they had arrived home by telling Barbara to call her if and when she felt like talking.

Reflecting on the events of the evening, Abigail began to weep. "I'm so sorry our evening turned into a nightmare, Ed. I feel it's my fault."

"Nonsense," he said. "We had no way of knowing what was going to happen."

"I know it was him or them or whatever," and she threw her arms up totally frustrated.

"I agree with you, Abigail. The pattern was the same. The assault came after the two calls, and if you remember, the pickup struck twice. It must be the same person." Then he started pacing for a moment, thinking. He stopped in front of Abigail. "Whoever it was must have been watching your apartment. How else would they have known what vehicle you were riding in," he deduced.

She didn't like the thought her unknown enemy had been watching her apartment. Not at all, and it was much too close. The mere thought sent a chill down her spine. She thought out loud. "What will his next move be, forced entry into my apartment? Can I expect bodily harm?" and her voice was stressed.

Ed took hold of her hands. "I'll protect you whenever I can. In the meantime, if you see anything suspicious, call 911. And keep your door locked at all times."

"I will," she said, and she gave him a squeeze. "I just want this day to be over. Let's go to bed. I just want to be held," and she took hold of his hand.

CHAPTER 12

Conrad had decided Ed's relationship with Abigail wasn't progressing fast enough. His desire and the waiting to see her get hurt had started to erode his patience. After all, Ed had told him he hadn't yet had sex with her. Sex would establish intimacy, which in turn would enhance emotion and feeling that would incubate love. At least that's the way he saw it. It was nine in the morning. He would go to the condo and see Ed, and there would be no phone call. Yes, his visit would be unannounced.

After ringing the doorbell several times, he became annoyed when Ed didn't answer. "Where the Christ is he?" he grumbled. "I'll go in and wait," he decided, and he opened the door with his key. Once inside, he walked around inspecting and observing the area. Everything was neat and orderly. There were no dirty dishes, and the bed was made. The condo was neat, much too neat. He didn't recall Ed Being a neat freak during their military days. He could only conclude that Ed wasn't spending much time at the condo, which raised the question, where was he spending most of his time? The answer was simple. He spent it at Abigail's apartment, and it didn't take a rocket scientist to figure it out.

"The scumbag is holding out on me," he grumbled. "But why?" he asked himself. "He's going to have a lot of explaining to do, a lot," he continued conversing with himself. He sat and watched television for a while, changing the channels frequently. He couldn't concentrate, and nothing seemed interesting.

After what appeared to be an eternity in time, he heard footsteps behind the door. "Finally," he said letting out a heavy sigh.

"I thought I'd let myself in," Conrad greeted him when he came through the door.

"I surmised that when I saw your car in the lot. How you doing, buddy?"

"This place is very neat, Ed. Neat and tidy," and Conrad by passed any small talk. "I find it strange. I don't recall you being the neatest person during our military days. As a matter of fact, I recall you placing a piece of tape on your civilian pants at the bottom of your fly to conceal a tear. I remember specifically it was a black piece of tape."

"Ed smiled. "I remember, buddy. I wouldn't do that now, of course. As to being neat, I guess Shelly rubbed off on me. She was an exceptionally neat and tidy individual. She was fastidious actually."

Conrad studied Ed for a moment as if evaluating what he had said. Then he walked to the window that faced the woodlands and stared out. "Have you and Abigail copulated?" and he continued to stare out the window.

Ed hesitated for a moment and Conrad said, "You know, have you screwed her yet?"

Ed coughed, and then coughed again as he cleared his throat. "We recently made love," and he felt relieved telling him.

"How was it?" he immediately asked.

"Good. It was very good," and he wondered when the questions would end.

Conrad turned from the window. "Was she satisfied?"

Ed felt uncomfortable now that Conrad was looking at him. He took a deep breath. "I would say yes, she was satisfied."

"Good, your relationship has been consummated. How much does she love you?"

He was acting out a role remember? So why was he hating the questions so much? And Ed thought, I know why, you fool. Your role has become personal. You now will take the fall with her, and how will you handle Conrad? Now his mind was racing. Oh, he felt so uncomfortable. He wished Conrad would stop with the interrogation.

"How much does she love you?" Conrad repeated.

"Enough, I guess," and the question and his answer made him feel awkward. "I really don't know how to measure it," and he shrugged his shoulders.

Conrad studied Ed for a moment giving him the distinct impression that Conrad enjoyed making him uncomfortable. Ed watched him pace and then be seated in a large armchair next to the fireplace. Conrad leaned back and rested his head against the cushion in a relaxed posture. "Quite frankly Ed, my patience waiting for this drama to end has run out. From what you say and don't say, I feel she is ready to take the fall," and his voice was calm.

The words made Ed's pulse quicken and his body felt warm. It was inevitable the time would eventually come for him to drive the stake of betrayal into Abigail's heart.

When he first accepted Conrad's offer, it seemed like an easy favor to perform. Conrad was distraught, after all, and he had felt compassion for his friend. Besides, he had not known anything about Abigail's character except that she had insensitively dumped Conrad. But things were different now. After acting out his role he had gotten to know and like her. Their relationship had developed into one of intimacy, and she had openly admitted she loved him. He had used the word love more sparingly, not because he didn't care about her, but to relieve the anxiety he would feel whenever he thought about having to end their relationship.

Now Conrad wanted him to end it, but his heart wasn't ready. With a new awareness he knew now it would never be ready. He decided to stall him.

Ed wiped his brow with his hand and seated himself opposite Conrad. "I don't think it's an appropriate time to breakup the relationship, buddy," said Ed. "Abigail is being harassed by some psychopath. The girl is terrified," and he wasn't sure how Conrad would react to the information.

Conrad's lips broke into a wry grin. "Is that so? I wonder whom the bitch pissed off now?" and he studied Ed for a moment. "Tell me more. What's this psychopath doing?"

"There have been two incidents so far. I'll put it succinctly. She receives two, high pitched, wailing phone calls with no conversation. A short time later something happens. The first time all four tires on her car were slashed. The second incident was more serious."

"Really," said Conrad, and he leaned forward in the chair. "Such as," and he gestured with his hand for Ed to continue.

"Last night we were going to have dinner with a couple of Abigail's friends at the restaurant by the landmark lighthouse. After we turned onto a junction from the main road, a short time later a pickup truck deliberately struck us in the back. Then it crashed against the side of her friends SUV a couple of times before we pulled off the road. It scared the hell out of everybody. Luckily, no one was injured."

Conrad was calm and expressionless. To Ed, he appeared indifferent to the incident. "Did you see who was driving the pickup?"

"Unfortunately it was too dark, and the rain didn't help matters. I have no idea who it was," and Ed tightened his lips in frustration.

"This psychopath can continue his harassment indefinitely, Ed. I just can't wait any longer. Abigail is a big girl, and she's going to have to deal with it herself," and he rose from the chair.

Ed was annoyed with his attitude. It was still another manifestation of the degree of his hatred for her. "I realize she hurt you buddy and that you're angry, but I'm sure you don't want anything harmful to happen to her," and he sincerely hoped Conrad would finally show some compassion. But he didn't.

"It sounds like she has a personal problem. She has control over her fate. We all have some degree of control over our fate. Don't let her drag you into hers."

Ed was becoming more distressed and anxious with every new line of conversation, and he could no longer hide his concern and apparent feelings for Abigail from Conrad. "To abandon her now would be indecent," Ed insisted.

"Bull shit," Conrad blurted. "Wait a minute," he continued, "you have become soft on her. How long have you been hot on her?" and his voice conveyed disgust.

Ed did not answer, and Conrad looked straight at him. "I'll construe your silence to mean you're hooked on her. Let me tell you Ed, you better unhook your ass fast," and his words were stern.

"I'm not a cruel person, Conrad," Ed spoke up. "It's impossible not to feel something in a relationship," Ed said in self defense.

"I can't believe we're having this conversation. We made a deal, or did you forget? You're an actor, and you were to play a role, not get caught up with the bitch in a real life drama. You will see her tonight and tell her it's over, Ed." Conrad paused and stared hard into Ed's eyes. "If you don't, I'll have to take matters into my own hands. Trust me, you don't want me to do that," and Ed took it as a threat.

He couldn't believe the magnitude of Conrad's hatred for Abigail. It had not abated with time, and on the contrary it seemed to persevere and strengthen. He couldn't handle another moment of Conrad's company. He would capitulate. "Okay, Conrad, I'll tell her tonight," unsure at the moment how he would react when he saw her later.

"Good, I'm happy to see your spirit of cooperation has returned. Don't let the bitch come between our friend-ship, Ed. If you ever became serious with her, she would screw you in the end too. I know her well, Ed," and Conrad was smiling now. "Call me early tomorrow. I'll be very anxious to hear all the gory details."

Ed was glad to see him leave. The conversation had left him with every nerve in his body battered, and he paced and took several deep breaths to bring his being back to normal. "Why did I agree to get involved in his plan in the first place," he lamented. And then he said with remorse, "What have I done."

When Conrad left Ed's condo, he decided to drive to eastern Norwalk to pickup some Italian pastry. The bakery was located in a mid to lower income area. It was an area his mother considered below the family dignity level and criticized him whenever he made his sporadic trips. But the pastry was superb, as he would refer to it, even if he had to listen to his mother's bitching, as he would call it.

His favorite pastry was cannolli, and he always had an insatiable desire to consume them. He was feeling depressed, and the cannolli would give him a lift.

When he came out of the bakery, a thin, frail looking girl had just placed a note on his windshield secured by a wiper blade. "Excuse me," she said meekly when she saw him. "I had no idea where you were, so I left a note. I'm so sorry I accidentally backed into your car," and her nervousness was reflected in her voice.

"Ah, shit," and she cringed with his words. "Let me see the freaking damage," and he walked to the rear of his car. The center of the rear bumper had a dent, and the bumper itself had been pushed in toward the body below the trunk.

"It's going to have to be replaced," he grumbled.

"I'm so sorry. I never had an accident before," she volunteered.

"Well, you have now, honey," and he was curt, making her more nervous. He scanned the note. "Penny Hennessey huh, and you're insured by Liberty Mutual of America. Let me see your driver's license," and her hand trembled when she handed it to him. "You're not quite twenty-one. Who taught you how to drive, your grandfather on his damn tractor?"

She took his cheap shot and said nothing in her defense.

"I see you listed your phone number. I'll call you after I have the damage assessed." He started for his care and stopped. "Where is your car?" he asked.

"Over there," and she pointed to a 1982 Plymouth with badly faded paint and several rust spots on the rear fenders.

When Conrad saw it he laughed. "Don't fix it if it has any damage. It belongs in the freaking junkyard," and his comment hurt her and made her eyes tear.

He started his car and made the tires squeal when he drove away.

Later that evening, Conrad was seated in one of the recliners in the family library. He was in his stocking feet and held a paperback book in his hand, but at the moment he wasn't reading. Instead his mind was occupied with the events of the accident that had transpired earlier in the day. His mind kept focusing on Penny Hennessey and her meek, timid demeanor, and her homely face and frail looking body. He recalled everything that had happened with no remorse or regret for what he had said. No, he was focusing on Penny Hennessey as an individual who he could capitalize on.

He placed his hands behind his head and closed his eyes, exerting his mental capacity relentlessly, pursuing, scheming a way to use Penny as a victim of revenge. She would be such a perfect candidate, so unsuspecting and innocent. Yes, he would pursue her and give her priority over Erica Hollis. It would be a crime to let Penny go unscathed. He would never be able to find such an excellent candidate like her again. He would work on the two of them simultaneously. There was no doubt he could handle his revised plan. The very thought energized his body. He opened his eyes and smiled.

He would call Penny and apologize for his harsh treatment of her and insist on paying his own damage, and take her to dinner. He would fatten her up with flattery and affection until she placed her heart in his hands, and then he would squeeze the life out of it. The thought made him grin, but in the end the homely, little bitch would cry.

CHAPTER 13

*E*d was spending most of his time at Abigail's apartment ever since her unknown enemy had increased the proximity and severity of the harassment targeted at her. As a result, her level of fear had increased commensurately, and he was more determined than ever to protect her.

With Abigail working and Ed out of work, they had established a routine where he would cook the evening meals most of the time. Food preparation was nothing new to him. He had worked as a cook on and off when he had been between acting jobs.

Abigail would be home shortly to join him for a dinner consisting of breaded pork chops, steamed broccoli and baked potato. During the time he was preparing dinner, Conrad's words insisting he tell her tonight he was breaking up with her kept reverberating in his head. His stomach was in knots and his appetite was abating by the minute. It made him resent Conrad all the more. He was toying with the thought that if he did do it, what would be the best approach to lessen the impact. Perhaps she would listen and understand if he was straight forward with the truth. And forgive him and still love him. How he hoped it would be the case. To relieve stress and tension, he reconciled himself to the fact she would understand why he foolishly would accept such a role. And he would beg her forgiveness. Oh yes, he would beg.

Abigail would be coming through the door any moment, and his head started to throb. He was developing a headache, and he could hear the sound of his pulse beating in his head. He was anxious, and he desperately tried to stay calm.

A moment later the doorknob turned and Abigail entered the apartment. "Hi, my darling," she greeted him. She kicked off her high, heel shoes and walked up to him and kissed him. "I love kissing you. Something smells good. I think I'll let you cook all the time."

He forced a smile. "Glad to be useful."

"You're very useful, my darling. You have a great pistol that fires a bull's eye all the time," and she waited for some kind of reaction.

He was slow reacting. "I get it."

She studied him for a moment. "You planning on going to the firing range later?" and she smiled.

He forced another smile and lagged his response; "If you supply the target," Abigail.

"I sure will. I have a tremendous stock pile," and she headed for the bedroom to change her clothing. Then she stopped and turned to face him. "You okay? You don't seem to be yourself."

No, he wasn't. He had to make a better effort to conceal his worry.

"My stomach is a little sour, but I'll survive."

"I hope so. Perhaps you'll feel better after you eat something," and she went into the bedroom.

A short while later they were seated opposite each other at the dinner table.

"I had an idea enter my head today while I was working," Abigail said as she served herself some broccoli. "A rather good one," she continued.

"Share it with me."

"It has to do with your acting talent. You did such a great job entertaining the children at the hospital. Your character little Laffy is good. Really good, and so adorable," she praised him.

"Keep going," he said. "I love the flattery."

"I'm serious, Ed. I think you should give the concept to some TV producers for a possible children's' show. I think it would fly," she said with robust enthusiasm.

He did enjoy doing shows with little Laffy, but he had never given consideration to what Abigail had suggested. "It's an interesting suggestion, and I'll give it serious consideration."

"You owe it to yourself, my darling. You're too good to go unnoticed as an actor. Why can't those damn agents do something positive for you?" she moaned, and her desire for him to be successful was blatant.

"It's a difficult road to travel, Abigail. It's full of obstacles and extremely competitive. Most of all, you have to have perseverance for any chance to make it."

"I guess you're right. It's just that I know how talented you are. So does Jennifer Sweet. You know, the broad who is hot on you," she teased.

"How could I forget such a strikingly, beautiful girl," and though he teased her back he meant it.

"See, I was right. You do like her," and though the mood of their conversation was one of teasing, she couldn't help feel Jennifer was a distant threat.

When they finished dinner, Ed had consumed half of his meal. The conversation with Abigail did help him momentarily lessen his focus on spilling the beans as to why he took on his deceptive role.

"I'll do the dishes," volunteered Abigail as she rose from the table. "You rest in the den, my darling. I want you to feel better," and she kissed him gently on the forehead.

"But I want to help."

"Go, now," and she pushed him gently toward the den.

A moment later he approached her in the kitchen. "Abigail, I have to talk to you about something serious," and she sensed something was wrong.

She studied him for a moment, and her facial expression was one of concern. "Is something wrong?" and she removed her hands from the dishwater.

"I . . ." and he hesitated.

"What is it?" and she stood in front of him and took hold of his hand. "Tell me. You know you can tell me anything," and she started to worry.

"I don't know," and he paused interrupted by the ringing of the phone.

They both turned and stared at the phone. "Maybe it's Barbara," and Abigail picked up the receiver. "Hello," she said hoping to hear Barbara's voice.

There was silence, and it prompted her to say hello again.

"Pray, pray, the devil's going to take him away, away," and the words were recited by a high, pitched voice. They were followed by the wailing sound she had heard before. Her nerves made her drop the receiver. "Oh, my God!" she cried, and she backed away from the phone as if it had the ability to harm her.

"What is it?" he immediately asked after seeing her reaction to the phone call. The scenario was all too familiar and he already knew the answer to his question. "It was the psychopath, wasn't it?"

"It was really horrible, Ed," and she took several deep breathes before continuing. "This time they talked."

"What did they say?" eager for her answer.

"They said," and she placed her hand on her chest between her breasts. "The voice said, pray, pray, the devil's going to take him away," and she was trembling.

He couldn't believe what was happening. It was one terrible event after another, and his mind started racing. He quickly decided he would ignore Conrad's threat and not burden her with a broken relationship. She had enough to handle with the son-of-a-bitch harassing her.

"I think they were referring to you, Ed." The more she thought about it the more convinced she became. "I'm frightened. I couldn't handle it if anything happened to you," and she hugged him tightly.

"Nothing will happen to me. I won't let it," he tried to assure her, and he meant it. He had had enough harassment from the faceless enemy plaguing them. He was tired of Conrad placing pressure on him to end his plotted relationship with her. With renewed determination he vowed to remain adamant to their threats, even if it came to exchanging bodily blows.

He made her sit down and drink some water to calm her nerves. "Now breathe deeply and blow out slowly."

She did as he said, and it made her feel less anxious. "Thank you, Ed," and she squeezed his hand and kissed it in appreciation.

Then she looked up at him with sad eyes. She was worried and said, "Who would want to take you away from me?" and she placed his hand against her cheek.

"I don't know. Are you sure that's what they said?"

"Oh, I'm sure. No mistake about it," and she wished she had heard wrong.

Ed thought a moment. There was one person he could think of who wanted to take him away, and that was Conrad. Could it be him? But why would he call and warn her? Could it be to frighten and harass her? He thought more. Was Conrad behind the other calls? He did hate her. Perhaps his daft behavior towards her gave him pleasure and satisfaction. But would he go so far as to risk seriously injuring Abigail and the other passengers with the car incident. He wished he knew the answers. Right now he could only speculate, and under the circumstances he had to keep his thoughts to himself.

Abigail broke his concentration. "What did you want to tell me, my darling? You seemed upset," and she was still seated.

He hesitated. "It's nothing," he lied. "It can wait."

"Are you sure?"

"I'm sure," and his answer with a lack of urgency seemed to pacify her.

He would confront Conrad in the morning after she left for work. Yes, confront him, and when he went to bed the thought made his body stir and caused him to waken several times during the night.

After Abigail left for work, Ed phoned Conrad and told him to meet him at the condo. Within the hour Conrad was there.

"Has the bitch taken her fall?" he immediately asked, and he headed for the chair next to the fireplace.

He seated himself, and to Ed, appeared to be rather calm in light of his opening remark.

Ed cleared his throat. "No, she hasn't," and Conrad could hear the nervousness in his voice.

"I'm not surprised, Ed. From what you said the other day, I surmised you no longer had the balls," and the comment angered Ed.

"It's not a matter of having balls. I have two, a perfect pair hanging properly, my friend," and he tried to remain calm. "It's a matter of having compassion. I told you before, the timing isn't right."

"You're fired, Ed. You have failed and betrayed me. You have let her win you over. Apparently, she has screwed your brain dry. You let her sexual appetite dominate you."

Ed let him talk, still puzzled by his calmness, even though his words were strong and bitter. Was it the calm before the storm? Did he have an alternate plan? All plotting warriors usually had a backup plan. He was convinced Conrad had one and suspected he would use it soon.

"Since you no longer work for me, I want you out of the condo as soon as possible. No, let me rephrase that. You have until tomorrow night. See, I'm not such a bad guy, Ed," and he gave him a wry grin. He continued, "I'm expecting some remuneration from you since you didn't carry out your assignment to a successful conclusion. I'll calculate an amount of pay for you before you leave," said Conrad, and he shifted his body in the chair. "Why don't you sit, Ed? You're ass on fire?"

"The scumbag," Ed said to himself. Conrad had a way of rattling his nerves. "Conrad," Ed said, "you ever considered forgiving Abigail and releasing all that hatred knotted inside of you? If you don't, it's going to take a toll on your health," he tried to plead with him.

"I'd rather die first than forgive that relentless bitch. I hate her more with each passing day. What would you know about it? You're out of it now. I'll handle it my way," and his face was flushed. The calmness he manifested previously was now gone. "I'll do whatever it takes to destroy the bitch," he rattled on.

Ed did not like hearing the word destroy, and Conrad was making him fearful of what could possibly happen to Abigail.

"Please, Conrad, won't you reconsider and forgive her?" he again tried to reason. "You're hatred has made you cross over to the other side of love. That's no place to dwell. Give yourself closure.

"Mind your freaking business, Ed. I'll handle my own problem. You're out of it, remember? Take my advice and leave Connecticut. You're finished here." He said no more and left slamming the door behind him, leaving Ed standing and wondering what was coming next.

CHAPTER 14

A few hours after his confrontation with Ed, an angry Conrad decided to see Abigail at her place of employment. He wanted to drop the bomb without further delay. It didn't matter where. He knew she was employed as a secretary to the Vice President of Marketing in a direct mail company. When she heard what he had to tell her, he surmised she more than likely would not return to work, and the thought of messing up the remainder of her day pleased him.

Conrad was in the lobby of Direct Inc. at eleven in the morning. Upon his arrival the receptionist was busy conversing with a client, and having to wait to address her started to get on his nerves. He was tapping on the floor with his foot while he waited. "Come on, quit the bull shit you scumbag," he said to himself.

When the client finally left he approached the receptionist. "I have an urgent message for Abigail McCloud. Would you please ask her to come to the lobby?"

"May I tell her who is calling, sir?"

No way was he going to give his name. The initial shock of her seeing him was part of his strategy. "She isn't expecting me. I want to surprise her. Just tell her someone is here to see her. Can you do that for me?" and he smiled.

She hesitated for a moment then said, "I guess its okay."

The receptionist picked up the phone and said, "You have a gentleman visitor," and then Conrad heard her say, "He didn't give his name. She will be right out, sir."

"Thank, you," and he seated himself in a chair next to a huge floor plant.

"It must be Ed," Abigail told herself when she was notified she had a visitor. When she entered the lobby and didn't see him, she was disappointed. Instead she noticed two men, one with a briefcase and the other occupied with reading a magazine. Neither one of them seemed to be concerned about her presence. Conrad sat unnoticed with his legs exposed but his torso hidden by the thick leaves and branches of the huge plant.

"Ann, has my visitor left?" Abigail asked most curious. Ann quickly leaned forward in her chair and scanned the lobby. "You're visitor is seated next to the floor plant," she informed her.

"Thank, you," and she started to walk toward the plant leaning her head to see around it. When she saw Conrad she stopped. "What are you doing here?" she asked instinctively.

He gave her a wry grin and said, "To see, you."

Her face immediately became flushed, and she felt warm. Being in his presence made her feel uncomfortable. She hadn't seen or communicated with him in three months, ever since she had ended their relationship. That's the way she had wanted it. Ed now had made her forget about any previous relationship. She was happy now, and her new relationship gave her a sense of fulfillment.

"What do you want to see me about?" she asked him, her voice tense.

"It's something very important," and he walked up to her and gently took hold of her arm. "I don't think you're going to want to talk here in the lobby," he whispered. "We should go outside."

She had no idea why he had come to see her at work and at such an early hour. No idea at all. She felt annoyed, puzzled and disturbed all at the same time. "Fine," she said to his request, and she accompanied him out the door.

"What's this all about, Conrad? I'm scheduled for a meeting with my boss shortly. So make it fast."

"I won't be able to do that," and he was enjoying keeping her in suspense and waiting.

"Why the hell not?" and her patience started to abate.

"Because I have a lot of mind, boggling information for you," he informed her.

"Such as what?" she snapped.

"Ed McDowell, your lover," and he gave her a hard stare.

"What?" and her mouth remained open. Her eyes fluttered from nerves and she took a real deep breath. "Did I hear you correctly?"

"Yes, you did," he said before she could say anything else.

"How… how do you know about him?" she stuttered, and her voice became stressed. "He never mentioned you."

"Why, he's an old army friend. He's working for me. I hired him to make your acquaintance and date you. Remember the flat tire? Good actor isn't he, but he has no balls. He was the one who was supposed to talk to you, but he chickened out."

It was all happening too fast. And it made sense. The more she thought about what he had just said, the more real and poignant her nightmare was becoming. "You son-of-a-bitch," she screamed at him, and when she went to slap his face he caught her arm with his hand.

"Temper, temper," he mocked her.

She was livid with him. She wanted to strike back at him and hurt him physically. His words were cutting into her heart.

"Your lover has betrayed you, Abigail, just like you betrayed me. Don't like it, do you? Vengeance is mine, sayeth Conrad," and he laughed loudly.

"You sick bastard," and she started to cry.

"Now you know how it feels. It hurts a great deal, doesn't it? It's like a monster ripping your heart out of your chest and leaving an empty cavity. It's an empty feeling that diminishes you more each day." He was spewing all his pent-up feelings as result of being dumped, as he had labeled it.

Ironically, all the emotion he expounded on, she herself started to feel. Oh, my God! Abigail thought, and her mind raced. Ed collaborated with Conrad. That beautiful man I have fallen in love with has been using me. The horrible realization Ed had been using her made her chest wretch with pain.

"You deserve everything you got, Abigail," and he said it with hatred.

She started to feel sick. "The phone calls. Did you make the phone calls?" she asked still crying.

"I'll never tell," and he flashed his wry grin.

Her sick feeling had peaked, and she moved hurriedly toward the shrubs by the side of the building. A moment later she vomited, and Conrad looked on with pleasure.

"My, God," she moaned. "I have to get out of here," and she headed for the parking lot.

"What's the matter, poor baby have a tummy ache?" he called after her. He watched her get into the car, raise the engine and blow out of the parking lot. "Damn, I think that broad should drive in the Indianapolis 500," he said facetiously.

He went back into the lobby and approached the receptionist. "I don't think Ms. McCloud is coming back to work." He leaned forward and whispered, "Men problems." He smiled at the receptionist and said, "Have a nice day." She watched him leave and grumbled, "Strange man."

It was late afternoon when Ed arrived at Abigail's apartment. He knew she was home when he noticed her car parked in its assigned space. But why was she home now? Ed wondered. She worked until five o'clock and usually arrived home at five-thirty. Perhaps something was wrong. He entered the apartment curious.

"Abigail, I'm home." When she didn't answer he headed for the bathroom. There was no sign of her. "The bedroom, she's in the bedroom," he told himself. When he came to the doorway he stopped. She was lying on her back with her forearm resting on her forehead. Her eyes were red with dark circles and puffy skin, the condition brought on by excessive crying. On the nightstand was a half empty bottle of rum.

"Conrad," he said to himself. "The low, life bastard got to her." He went into the bedroom. He had to talk to her and clear the air. "Abigail, this is Ed, and I have to talk to you."

She opened her eyes and stared at him. Her body was relaxed from the consumption of rum. The stress from the confrontation with Conrad had sapped a great deal of her body strength, and she was visibly exhausted.

"I know everything, Ed. You don't have to try to defend yourself. Just leave," and she turned her head away from him. "I'm so tired now. Leave me in peace. At least do that much for me. I just want to die."

She was breaking his heart. He felt like his life was suddenly engulfed in a pocket of gloom. He did love her, but how could he ever make her believe it now. He had to try.

"Abigail, please believe that I'm in love with you. I know you don't want to talk to me now, but please give me a chance to explain what happened," and he was frantic.

She started to sob. "How can I believe anything you say? It's over, Ed. Please let me sleep and never wake up again. Now, please let me sleep," and she slurred the word sleep.

He watched her close her eyes and fall into a peaceful slumber. Then he placed a blanket over her suspecting she would sleep the night. He stared at her and his eyes started to tear. How awful he felt, and he hated himself for what he had done. He knew he could never forgive himself. No, he never could. Oh, how he wished he could pick her up and hold her and make all the hurt go away. Make things right and good the way they were before.

He decided he would stay the night and sleep on the couch. She would feel better physically in the morning and he would be able to talk to her. He would beg her to listen.

When Abigail awoke in the morning, she had a hangover. It was after she had a glass of tomato juice she realized Ed was in the apartment. "What are you doing here?" and she was curt. "I want you to leave."

"Abigail, please give me a chance to explain. I don't know what Conrad told you. All I know is that I love you, and I ask you please hear my side of the story," and there was urgency in his voice.

"Ed, listen to me carefully. You lied to me and used me, two terrible things to do to a person. Most of all, you betrayed me. Nothing you do or say can change that, and I'll hurt for the rest of my life. There is nothing to discuss." She was reliving all too soon yesterday's vile encounter with Conrad, and she started to sob.

"I'm sorry, Abigail," he again apologized. "I didn't mean to upset you. I…"

"I can't be with you now," she interrupted him. "I'm angry and hurt. I'll probably never stop loving you, but I don't think I can ever forgive you." She paused for a moment. "I really want you to leave now," and she wiped the tears from her face.

He looked at her face as if to permanently engrave the image in his memory. Even in sadness she was beautiful, and her eyes sparkled from the water of her tears.

Regretfully, he would honor her request, and a feeling of helplessness swarmed over him. His chance to explain how he felt would be circumvented by her scared emotions. "I love you, Abigail," he said before he exited her apartment. He refused to succumb to the thought he had lost her. If only he had talked to her before Conrad had punctured her jugular vein with his ruthless fangs. If only he had been honest with her the other night. If only he had, had, and he tormented himself by thinking about it again and again.

When he got into his car and started to drive, he realized he had no place to go. He had already vacated the condo and Abigail's apartment was off limits. He had to think, and the park would be the perfect place. He found a bench a distance away from where the ducks were congregated, and after sitting a while he felt shaky and then realized he hadn't eaten breakfast or dinner the night before.

He could go without food, but being alienated from Abigail was killing him.

He sat back on the bench and closed his eyes to relive in his mind all the good times they had shared, and he wanted his life with her back.

When he opened his eyes, he noticed a young couple holding hands strolling nearby. They stopped and kissed, looked at each other lovingly, and then continued walking. It was the epitome of love and contentment, and he hankered for the same.

After observing the lovers, he decided he would stay at a local motel to give Abigail time to reassess her feelings. Then he could call her and perhaps she would be receptive to seeing him. He would give her a week. It sounded good, and that would be his plan.

By the end of the second day he was going out of his mind with boredom, and he was so restless he could literally jump out of his skin. He couldn't really concentrate on anything, and his sleep was restless at best. He missed talking to her, and the way she made passionate love. And he missed falling asleep holding her warm, tender body. What bothered him the most was the fact he never had the opportunity to express his feelings over what had happened. She didn't want to see him anymore, but maybe she would feel differently if he could only talk to her. One thing was sure. Without her he felt like he was living in hell.

When the sun set behind streaks of clouds in the western sky on the fifth day of Ed's stay in Fairfield for the purpose of giving Abigail time to assess her feelings, he decided it was time to communicate with her. Besides, he had run out of patience. What would happen next would probably permanently alter the direction of his life.

Before he dialed the phone he took several deep breaths to stabilize his breathing. Then he waited anxiously for her to pickup the receiver. On the fifth ring he heard her say, "Hello." The sound of her voice was like the sweetness of music from a divine harp emanating from billows of heavenly, white clouds high in the sky.

He couldn't believe how nervous he was. He was so nervous his veins tingled. "Abigail, this is Ed," and he waited for her to acknowledge him.

After what appeared to be an eternity, she said, "Hello, Ed."

It was a start. She hadn't hung up. "How are you, Abigail? I miss you so much."

A moment later to his relief, she responded, "I miss you too." Her disenchantment and hurt had obviously mellowed, and apparently she didn't hate him. He felt more positive about the situation and it made his confidence soar.

"Would it be okay if I stopped by? I really need to talk to you."

"I'd like that," she said softly.

"Thank you, Abigail. I really appreciate it, and I'll see you soon."

On the way to see her, he stopped at a florist and charged a dozen long stemmed, yellow roses. The least he could do for her forgiving and understanding nature.

When he rang the bell to her apartment, he suddenly felt nervous, and his emotions of shame and guilt couldn't be denied. When he saw her, however, his body became void of all emotion except joy. She was beautiful, and he just wanted her back in his life. He stared at her adoringly and she said, "The flowers are beautiful. I'm assuming they are for me."

"I love you, Abigail," were the first words he wanted to say, and he hugged her tightly. He held her for a long time before he kissed her on the forehead. "I'm so sorry for everything that has happened. Please let me explain or my conscience will never be at peace."

She gave him a weak smile and nodded.

"Please sit next to me, Abigail, and listen with your heart."

Once they were seated, he started to talk. He went over the scenario from the beginning to his last conversation with Conrad. In the process of explaining, he stressed he had fallen in love with her early in their relationship, and all his actions of commitment were genuine and self motivated and not merely playing out a role. He emphasized he regretted accepting Conrad's proposition of deception, but not the time he had spent with her. In explaining he mentioned an upside to the affair was that it gave him the opportunity to make her acquaintance, and he would always be grateful for that. Yes, he had explained it all, and he could only hope she would believe him and find the capacity in her heart to forgive him.

"If you ever forgive me, it will probably be long before I forgive myself," he said. "I don't ever want to be separated from you again."

She reached for his hand and squeezed it. "I believe you, Ed. I want you in my life too. I'm sure in time we'll both be healed, and what has happened will be a memory of the past. Where are you staying?" she asked.

"At a motel; I no longer have the condo," and he felt awkward.

"I can do something about that. Would you like to stay with me?" she offered. Oh, how grateful he was she had offered.

"I accept," he quickly replied, and he took her into his arms. They were back together, and they both thought, life is going to be beautiful again.

CHAPTER 15

Conrad was gloating over believing he had destroyed Ed and Abigail's relationship. He felt so good about it that he was anxious to set up his next victim and then work on her ultimate demise. He looked at himself in the mirror, pointed and said, "Penny Hennessey, I nominate you," and he laughed with the intensity of an insane person. He already had Erica Hollis on one hook, and he would soon have another fish, Penny Hennessey on another hook. He was smart enough to know he would have to bait Penny differently than Erica. After his brief exposure to her at the scene of the accident, he was able to deduce that Penny was terribly timid and introverted in contrast to Erica who was extroverted and confident.

His initial strategy would be one of gentleness and kindness. He had to win her confidence so she would go out with him. Then he would accelerate the tempo and give her a taste of life she had never experienced.

Conrad had moved into the condo vacated by Ed. He would need privacy to court his victims, especially when it became necessary to take them to bed. Everything was in place and it was time to act.

It was seven in the evening, and a good time to call Penny and drop the bait. He dialed her phone and she answered. "Penny, this is Conrad, the guy whose car you backed into."

She hesitated, and he could hear her breathing accelerate. "Yes, I remember," she said nervously.

"Well, I want you to relax. I'm the bearer of good news. First, I want to apologize for the harsh way I treated you. Actually, I am ashamed of myself. You didn't deserve that. I was having a bad day."

She didn't make a sound. "Are you still there?" he asked.

"Yes." Everything he was saying took her by surprise, and she could only listen.

"Good, because I have more good news," he informed her. I've decided I'm going to pay for the repairs to both our cars."

It was getting better, and she couldn't believe what she was hearing. "Are you serious?" she asked not able to conceal her surprise.

"I sure am, but there is one small catch. You must let me take you to dinner to prove my apology is sincere and that you accept it. What do you say? Is it a deal?" and he speculated she would accept.

She hesitated before she answered. "I thank you for your dinner offer, but I haven't dated in a long time. I'm afraid I wouldn't be very comfortable."

"I promise I won't bite. If it will make you feel better, I'll go to the vet and have my fangs removed," and as nervous as she was, the remark made her laugh.

She pondered his invitation, but she was terrified to say yes. She knew nothing about him, and she was so nervous at the time of the accident she hadn't noticed his good looks and athletic build.

"I'll buy you anything you desire to eat," he interrupted her thinking. "I'll even buy you the restaurant if it will persuade you to say, yes," and he made her laugh again. "Please say yes," he begged knowing if he didn't get her to accept now it would be increasingly difficult to lure her later.

He could hear her breathing was more relaxed, and he construed her silence and delay in answering him as an indication she was giving his dinner invitation serious thought. Finally she said, "Yes, I'll go."

"Wonderful," he said with delight. "Is tomorrow evening at eight okay?"

"Yes, I'll be ready," and she wasn't sure she had made the right decision. She would never know how truly delighted he was, or why.

Penny Hennessy looked at herself in the mirror, something she did not like doing, making sure she looked respectable for her date. Yes, her date. She didn't remember the last time she had gone out with a member of the opposite sex. She only knew it had been a long time.

Penny was a realist, and she was well aware of her limited, physical endowments. She was twenty years old, and for the longest time she had felt that God, for some horrible reason, had chosen not to endow her with the more conventional and certain special qualities most other girls possessed. The texture of her hair was coarse at best, and it was the color of dirty sand. It always lacked luster even after she experienced exhausting trials of highly, advertised products that promised the impossible, at least where she was concerned. She was also thin and frail looking with undersized breasts. Her tiny eyes were a dull gray and unexciting. Even her complexion left a lot to be desired. Her skin gave the appearance that it had been continually deprived of sunlight and oxygen, making it pale and listless. Numerous, tiny pimples were clustered on her chin and on the sides of her small, narrow lips. Not even makeup could enhance her appearance. In the aggregate, Penny could best be defined as an unattractive, homely female. It was as simple as that.

To the observer it would appear that Penny had enough of a burden to carry in life dealing with the consequences that came with her unattractiveness, but unfortunately that wasn't where it ended. In addition to being homely, she had health problems. She caught colds easily and she was asthmatic. She had difficulty hearing in one ear, and recently she had been detected with a heart murmur. But she took all of it in stride, clinging to the belief that some day she would be the recipient of some divine blessing that would alter her life forever and make it a part of paradise. She fantasized often, perhaps the only way to make her current life tolerable. She was extremely sensitive and shy brought on by her insecurity, and it bred loneliness and emptiness in her life that caused her many a night to cry herself to sleep.

Penny turned away from the mirror and looked at her watch. It was almost eight in the evening and Conrad would be arriving any moment, and she had a feeling he would be punctual. She suddenly felt extremely nervous. She tried to calm herself by thinking it was a one time dinner date. Actually, it really wasn't a date in the true sense of the word. She was being foolish, very foolish. They would go out, talk a little and eat, and it would be over, and the night would be finished.

Feeling satisfied with her appearance, she started to walk down the staircase and before she reached the landing she heard the sound of the doorbell. She had guessed right about Conrad's punctuality, and it made her feel good.

When she opened the door, her eyes marveled at the dozen yellow roses Conrad held in his hand. They so absorbed her attention she did nothing but stare at them.

"Hello, Penny," Conrad finally said breaking her concentration.

"Hi," she said unable to cover her embarrassment for not greeting him. "The flowers, they…"

"I know, they're beautiful," he interrupted her trying to ease her embarrassment. "They're for you," and he handed them to her with a smile.

"They are so beautiful, and I thank you so much." No one could have been more sincere with a thank you. She had never received yellow roses from anyone before. Actually, the only flowers she had ever received were on her twentieth birthday from her sister Mindy.

"I should put them in water," and she started for the kitchen when she suddenly stopped and turned. "I'm sorry, Conrad, would you like to come in for a moment while I get a vase?"

"Sure," he said, and he observed how nervous and flustered she was. The flowers obviously had taken her by surprise and contributed to her awkward, nervous behavior.

When he stepped into the house he was in the living room, which was small and crowded with furniture. It all looked worn, and the carpet was definitely overdue to be replaced. A woman knitting sat in a chair in the farthest corner of the room. Next to her was a walker. He acknowledged her presence when she looked in his direction by nodding his head and smiling. Her mother, he guessed.

Penny returned to the living room with the vase of roses and placed them on a table next to the sofa. "Aren't they beautiful, mom?" she said, her voice proud.

"Lovely, dear," and she looked at Conrad.

"Oh," Penny sighed. "I'm sorry, mom. This is Conrad," and when he walked toward her mother Penny said, "Conrad, this is my mom."

"Hello, Mrs. Hennessey. I'm pleased to meet you," and he shook her hand.

"Nice meeting you. You and Penny have a nice evening," and it was blatantly obvious she was pleased her daughter was going out.

"Thank you, madam. I'm sure we will, and I won't keep her out late," and he smiled. Not this time. He had to be the perfect gentleman. Everyone had to like him. His plan had to work to perfection. How else could she feel the maximum pain?

When they were in Conrad's Trans Am he said, "Ready for some good food?"

"Yes," she answered, but her stomach was in knots.

He looked at her and smiled. "Any particular food you feel like eating tonight?"

"Not really. You choose, if you don't mind," and she didn't dare select an establishment. She assumed he was of decent financial means by the type of car he was driving, and more importantly, by the statements and comments he made during their few conversations.

"Okay, I'll choose for the both of us," and she was relieved. "I'll take you to a place where they do great, home style cooking. There's bound to be something you'll like."

"Thank you," and she thought, maybe he's not such a bad guy after all. He appears to be considerate of my feelings.

It was a half hour drive to the Fine Kettle Restaurant. Conrad kept the conversation to a minimum trying to give her a chance to unwind and settle down her nervous system. And he thought, after she had a few glasses of wine, it should abate any remaining signs of her anxiety.

On the outside the restaurant looked average and conventional, and the atmosphere on the inside was up scale and rich in country style. Penny liked it immediately, and her eyes started to roam focusing on the furnishings and some of the people dinning. Several of the patrons were well-dressed wearing jewelry that sparkled with the lighting.

When the hostess approached them, Conrad immediately requested a table in a more private section of the dining area. "Of course, Mr. Hill," he was acknowledged, and Penny wondered how the hostess knew his name. After they were seated, Conrad asked, "Is everything okay with you, Penny?"

"I'm fine," and she was amazed how much better she felt. Her nerves had subsided some, and the fine aroma of food started to stimulate her appetite.

Conrad studied her for a moment. "I hope I get to know all about you before the evening is over. I very much would like us to become friends," and he gave her a warm smile.

She shyly looked away, his words catching her by surprise. She had no idea he would have any desire to become acquainted with her. None, at all, and the thought totally aroused her curiosity. "There is very little to know about me. I have a very simple life," she said.

"Ah, that may be true, but still a life. Simple can be good. Definitely less complicated, and I'm sure it has its advantages. Ah, the waiter is here."

"May I get you something to drink?" the waiter asked.

Conrad made a gesture to Penny to order and she hesitated.

"Perhaps you'd like some wine with your dinner," Conrad said. She nodded approvingly.

"Good, that settles it. We'll have a bottle of your best Cabernet Sauvignon."

"Thank you, sir," and the waiter left.

"If you'd rather have a cocktail, it's no problem. I can…"

"The wine is fine, Conrad," she interjected realizing he was trying to accommodate her, trying to make her more comfortable. And she appreciated it. It also made her realize her uneasiness and awkwardness were still very prevalent in her behavior. She would have to try harder at becoming more positive with her demeanor. After all, if her behavior made her an awkward freak all evening he definitely would not ask her out again.

The waiter returned with the wine and poured some in each of their glasses. Then he took their orders for Pot Roast, one of the house specialties.

Conrad raised his glass and extended it toward Penny. "I propose we drink to the development of a mutually, enjoyable friendship," and he smiled at her.

Penny raised her glass and softly touched his. She had never been toasted before, and she could only construe he was becoming more determined to have a relationship with her as the evening progressed. The thought pleased her, but also raised a significant question. Why would he? Originally he had said he wanted to make amends for his mistreatment of her by taking her to dinner. Now he was advocating they engage in a friendship. He was handsome with a strong personality, and there probably wasn't a girl around that would refuse to go out with him. And she certainly had been in front of a mirror enough times to know how other people saw her physical appearance. So, confused she was.

"Tell me, Miss Hennessey, do you have any brothers or sisters?" he addressed her.

"I have an older sister Mindy, but she looks nothing like me," and the tone of her voice was indicative of self-disparagement.

"Do you have a good relationship?"

"Yes, we do. Mindy always stuck up for me ever since we were kids. She was always so protective," and she sipped some wine. "She still is, actually."

"Hey, she wants to protect her baby sister. There is nothing wrong with that. I have no one to protect me. I'm an only child. I believe my parents preferred having zero children, but somehow they screwed up their timing and produced me," and she sensed he was serious by the tone of his voice.

"Why do you say that?"

"My parents and I don't get along. We share different philosophies on life. The good thing is I no longer have to depend on them for support. My grandfather, God bless him, set me up with a large trust fund. He also willed my parents a small fortune. Of course, you would never know by the way my parents talk." He paused for a moment and drank some wine, then continued. "My mother accredits all their wealth to the hard work of my father and his land development corporation. And she thinks she is Mrs. Wall Street with her damn investments. Funny thing is she does make money," and he shook his head in a mood of disgust.

She felt sorry for him. She had her own problems with life and knew how painful it could be, especially when there was nothing one could do to resolve the burden. At least she had a sister and parents that loved her and cared about what happened to her. He obviously had no family member to talk to and confide in. She wondered if he was currently involved with a girl in a close relationship, but of course she would dare not ask.

The waiter brought their entrees and said, "Enjoy your dinner."

"It looks so good," Penny commented. She felt more relaxed after conversing with Conrad. He seemed less intimidating and less infallible since life also confronted him with problems. Her appetite was more intense, and she was genuinely hungry.

"Enjoy your dinner," he told her. After tasting it she said, "It's excellent, and I thank you."

He nodded and smiled. "It's my pleasure."

After a short period of silence Conrad spoke, "Penny, your sister Mindy, does she live at home with you?"

"No, she is married. She was lucky to meet a real nice guy."

"So will you. Just be patient," and he winked his eye.

"I'm afraid I'm going to have a long wait. Mindy is a very attractive girl. She dated regularly. I know I'm at a disadvantage. I have accepted what I am a long time ago," and she said it calmly.

He studied her for a moment. "Hey, physical appearance isn't everything. It's what you have in here that counts," and he brought his fist against his heart. "I have come across some beautiful girls that are snakes in the grass. Some so ruthless that they have no hearts, or if they do they are cast in stone."

It was the first time she heard him speak with such intensity, and she could hear his voice was bitter.

"Such beauty is wasted if there is no compassion or personality to go with it," he continued. "Believe me, I speak for most men."

His words made her feel good. He seemed to be sincere and talking from experience. She would work on improving her personality, making it more positive and upbeat. It would be a step in the right direction.

Conrad filled their wine glasses emptying the bottle. "So tell me, Penny, if I wanted to pursue a serious relationship with you would I have to clear it with Mindy the protector?"

She looked at him for a moment trying to decide if he was serious or joking. "I… I guess in the long run it would depend on how serious it really was," she said assuming he was more serious than joking with the question considering what remarks he had made earlier. Then she suddenly chuckled holding her napkin to her mouth.

It prompted him to ask, "What's so funny? Did I miss something?"

"I'm sorry, I was just thinking of Mindy and what she did when we were kids," and she laughed again.

"Please tell me. I really want to hear about it."

"Okay, but I hope I don't bore you."

"Absolutely not," and he was eager to hear what she had to say.

"Mindy was very athletic as a child. She frequently would play ball with the boys. One day I also wanted to play, but they refused to let me," and she was talking more freely now, the affect of the wine relaxing her mood. "When I insisted, they called me a skinny, ugly excuse for a girl. When Mindy heard them and saw me cry, she went off the wall. She picked up a stone and hurled it at the group leader, who was the one that had initiated the insults, and struck him in the forehead. When he came over to her she threatened to beat him up and he backed off."

"No," Conrad said amazed. "She did that?"

"She did," and he believed her.

"Wow, no wonder you're fond of her. She's quite the ally."

"Another time," Penny continued, "that same boy called me pimple face. I cried and went running home. When Mindy found out, she jumped him and beat him up. He never bothered me again."

"Interesting," he said.

She studied him for a moment. "You know, I haven't divulged that information to too many people."

"Then I should feel honored you confided in me."

"I guess."

He understood perfectly why she wouldn't want to reveal the information. After all, the conditions prompting the name calling then still persisted. She was skinny by definition, and she still had an abundance of pimples on her chin and the surrounding area. No one liked to repeat disparaging remarks about themselves.

They had eaten themselves full. Penny refrained from having dessert and Conrad had a piece of cheesecake. While they waited for the check, Conrad asked, "Where do you work, Penny?"

"I'm employed at the Corrugated Box Company. It's a twenty minute drive from my house."

"And what do you do?"

"I do accounts payable invoicing."

"You must work with a computer most of the time."

"All day, and it gets boring," and she emphasized boring.

"Well, it's a job. Some people don't have one," he said trying to make her feel better about hers.

"I do realize that. I don't mean to sound ungrateful, but it's very repetitious work. That's why I read during my lunch hour. I really love to read. It removes me from work and the routine of my life," she confessed.

"Let me guess," said Conrad, and he paused thinking, trying to determine what she preferred reading. "I say you read a lot of romance novels. The kind where a girl gets swept off her feet by some handsome guy, and they live happily ever after."

She moved in her seat and looked away and appeared to be a little uncomfortable.

"Am I right?" he asked.

"Yes, you are," she said softly. "How did you know?"

"Gut feeling," but it was more than that. She had all the symptoms that spoke out telling him she sought the world of fiction and romance where she could lose herself, and fantasize beyond the boundaries of reality and become any character she desired.

The waiter came with the check and Conrad immediately placed a credit card on the tray. It was only a matter of moments when the waiter returned to the table and returned the credit card to Conrad and replied, "Please sign here sir." Conrad signed the paper, and as he handed it to the waiter he said, "You did a fine job, and this is for you." Penny couldn't help but notice that he had given the waiter $30, and she wondered if someday she would ever be in a position to tip so freely.

When they were in the car, Conrad said, "I enjoyed having dinner with you, Penny. I'd like to take you out again if you're not involved with anyone. I got the impression that you're not, but I just want to make sure."

He had hinted during dinner about pursuing a relationship with her, but that's all it was, a hint. Now he was asking and her heart started to race. "Yes, I'd like that," and her nerves made her cough.

"That's good, and I'll be calling you soon," he said with a smile.

Her pulse raced during the entire drive home from the excitement she was feeling. She was going out again with a handsome guy of good, financial means. Yes, Penny Hennessey who some people frowned upon. She couldn't wait to tell her mother about her new friend.

When they had arrived at her house, he escorted her to the front door, and gave her a soft kiss on the cheek.

"Good night, Penny," and she watched him walk to his car and drive away. For a moment she stood by the front door to convince herself her evening was for real and not a dream.

CHAPTER 16

Conrad's dinner date with Penny had come to an end. With that, he no longer was focused on her. Instead, he refocused on Ed and Abigail. He already was on the road, and instead of returning to the condo he decided to drive by Abigail's apartment to check things out. He had to be sure she had thrown Ed out of her life even though he was convinced she had. But he had a lingering curiosity that had to be addressed. He wanted to see if her car was there and how many windows were lit in the apartment. Most of all, he had to see if there was any sign of Ed's car. It was eleven-thirty, and if he had any plans of spending the night with Abigail the car more than likely would be there.

When Conrad was within the last couple of miles of the apartment, he started to feel a little anxiety. What if the bitch somehow had forgiven him and they were back together. What if she had, and the mere thought angered him and made him breath faster. Yes, the mere, sickening thought.

He was now a quarter of a mile away. One stop sign and one turn, then he would be able to see. When he reached the apartment he parked across the street. From his vantage point he could clearly see the windows to the main living area and her bedroom. All the windows were lit with the exception of the bedroom.

"Now to see if the scumbag's car is around," Conrad mumbled to himself. He got out of the car and headed for the parking lot.

The lighting in the area was in moderation, and he quickly started searching for Ed's car. He searched two rows and no car, which pleased him. When he started another section further back he immediately saw it, and he suddenly felt like someone had hit him in the pit of his stomach with a hard fist. "That no good bastard," he said enraged, and he kicked the side of the car hard with his foot. His first instinct was to race to the apartment and have it out with the two of them, but that wouldn't be good enough. Something much more decisive had to be done, something severe and permanent. His anger was making his mind race.

He took several deep breathes in an attempt to calm himself. He had to be calm to think properly. More deep breathes and his breathing became somewhat normal. He walked briskly from the lot to his car, and once inside rested his head against the headrest. "I don't believe this," he said out loud. "That bitch can't win. She can't beat me," and his anger was again intensifying. He glanced at the apartment windows, which were now dark. "The bastards now must be making love," he lamented, and then pounded the side window of the car with his fist. It was too much to tolerate, and his body was shaking from anger. "I'm out of here," he said, and he started the car and hit the accelerator hard, making the tires squeal shattering the stillness of the night.

When Conrad was back in the condo, the first thing he did was make a drink, loading the glass with vodka with just a splash of orange juice. He downed it quickly and made himself another. Then he cussed at Abigail and Ed before seating himself in the large armchair next to the fireplace. He rested his head back on the cushion and tried to relax his body so he could think. He had to retaliate and he had to come up with how, otherwise he wouldn't be able to sleep.

At first, he thought about what he could do himself. Then he thought who could help him and offer assistance, or act in his behalf. A moment later the name Franco Botti came into his head. Like Ed, Conrad had made his acquaintance in the military. Franco had told him in private that if he ever had the need for serious help he was the one who could help him resolve the problem. He had informed Conrad he had good family connections in Brooklyn, New York and Providence, Rhode Island that were perfectly capable of eradicating any source of trouble quickly for a fee and without a trail. It sounded like the perfect solution to his problem.

He had kept Franco's phone number even though he doubted at the time he would ever need it. Now he would find out how serious Franco Botti had been.

He felt better knowing he would make the call in the morning. He would finish his drink and go to bed.

At ten the next morning, Conrad went to a pay phone to make his call. He was relieved when he heard Franco's voice say hello.

"Franco, this is Conrad Hill from the military. How are you?"

"Conrad, is it really you?" and he was genuinely pleased to hear from him.

"Sure is."

"I'm fine, and it's great hearing from you. Hey, I bet you need a favor," he guessed. "The type only I can perform."

"Very close. I need to talk to you," and Franco sensed urgency in his voice.

"Is there a park nearby where we can meet?' asked Franco.

"County Park in Fairfield," Conrad informed him.

"Give me a landmark, and tell me when you want me there." He was brief and to the point.

"In the general vicinity of the duck pond," said Conrad. Can you make it tomorrow?" Conrad pushed.

"It must be important. Tomorrow around noon sound okay?"

"That's great, and thanks, Franco."

"I'll see you tomorrow," and the phone disconnected.

He had made contact with Franco. Now things could fall into place. Apparently, everything Franco had told him back in the military was true. It appeared he did have the connections and means to carry things out, and Conrad couldn't wait for tomorrow to come.

The pain and hurt, along with the shock Abigail had felt from Conrad's revelation of his plotted conspiracy with Ed against her, had abated to the point where she and Ed enjoyed a new relationship. Even though her heart would always carry a scar from the incident, she loved him too much not to have him be a part of her life. She was totally convinced she was destined to become Mrs. Ed McDowell.

On the other hand, there was nothing more that would please Ed than having Abigail as his wife. But he wasn't convinced they had seen the last of Conrad. Ed hated to admit it, but it worried him. He knew Conrad had crossed the line to the other side of love, and he doubted if he would ever cross back.

Abigail had gone to work and he was alone in the apartment. After he tidied up, he decided he would surprise her by preparing dinner. She liked Italian, and he would begin with Fusilli, her favorite type of pasta, a tossed salad with his own version of garlic dressing, hot, crisp Italian bread topped with garlic powder and parmesan cheese. And for dessert, he would run out to the market and pick up some Spumoni ice cream. Of course, a bottle of red wine was just understood. It sounded wonderful, and he hoped she would be pleased.

Later in the evening, they would retreat into the bedroom and make passionate love by candlelight. Yes, it sounded so wonderful. The least he could do for the pain he had caused her. He truly felt he could never do enough for her to make up for his actions, never.

At five-thirty Ed had the meal prepared with the exception of cooking the pasta. He wanted it to be al dante, firm the way Abigail liked it. Once she was home, he would simply place the pasta into the water, which was already boiling.

A moment after the clock announced it was five-thirty Abigail came through the door, punctual as usual. "Hi, my darling," she greeted him. The aroma made her say, "Aren't you the nice guy. You cooked dinner. Italian, how could I miss." She immediately gave him a kiss and said, "I love you."

"And I love you, Abigail," returning the words of affection.

"Excuse me while I get out of this dress."

"Sure, and take your time. Dinner won't be ready for another ten minutes."

He could see she was truly happy again, and he wanted her to feel that way forever. But for some uncanny reason he had been feeling an undertow of fear creeping through his body that he couldn't deny. And there was no way in hell he would mention it to her.

Abigail came out of the bedroom in a pair of shorts and a large, button shirt that draped down the length of her shorts. "Now I'm comfortable and ready for anything that comes my way," and Ed smiled at her as he poured the pasta in a colander.

"Sit, my beauty; salad and pasta coming up."

They seated themselves and began to eat.

"Delicious salad, my darling," and she wasted no time complementing him. "I think I'll turn the kitchen duties over to you, at least until you locate some work."

As they ate, Abigail said, "When you do another children's show for Jennifer Sweet, I'm going to inform the local TV station. Perhaps I can convince them to do a public interest piece for the evening news. Think of the exposure you could get. Good idea?" and she felt her idea was worthy of praise.

"You're good, Abigail, always thinking and aggressive. It's a good idea," and he wondered why he hadn't thought of it. He was aware she had mentioned before that his act would make a good television show for children. And it pleased him to know she thought his act was worthy enough to be made into a television production, and how extremely supportive she was. Shelly had never felt that way.

"I have another idea," she said after consuming a mouthful of pasta.

"You're full of ideas today. Go ahead and put the word on me."

"Why don't I take a day off from work and go to New York with you and see if some agencies can help you." She studied him for a moment. "I hope you don't think I'm being pushy, my darling. I don't mean to be."

"No, Abigail, I don't. You are right. I do want to work, and I have to admit I get discouraged at times."

"I happen to believe in you, Ed. You're good, and it upsets me that your talent isn't recognized." She admittedly was bias, but striving to be objective.

"Ready for some spumoni?" he asked, temporarily breaking the flow of conversation about his joblessness.

"Yes, I am." She loved it as much as he did.

When he was again seated he said, "I'll take you up on the New York offer. I'll set up some appointments."

"That's wonderful, and I'll be the woman behind the man. I relish the role."

They did the dishes together, at times splashing each other. To the observer, no one would have suspected the relationship had been in serious jeopardy a short time ago. When the dishes were done they sat in front of the television and relaxed for a while. Then as their eyes met, they didn't have to speak a word. They went into the bedroom where Abigail prepared the bed and Ed opened the drawer of the nightstand to take out some matches to light the candles. "Damn, we're out of matches," he moaned. "I really wanted us to have candlelight. If you don't mind, I'll run down to the convenience store and get some."

"If it's that important to you, my darling, then go. I'm not going anywhere. You hurry back now."

"You bet," and he threw her a kiss. "Be right back."

She loved when he was romantic, and she considered herself fortunate to have met him even after what had happened. And the irony was she had Conrad to thank. Life was certainly strange and unpredictable.

Ed would be back soon, so she went into the bathroom to freshen up. As soon as she came out the phone rang. Perhaps it's Barbara, she thought. Barbara had left a message on her answering machine earlier about her and Roy coming over to the apartment. It would mark the first time they had gotten together since the incident on the highway that had strained their friendship.

She picked up the phone and said, "This is Abigail." There was no response. Seconds later she heard the wretched, high pitch wailing sound she was all too familiar with. It was immediately followed by a distorted voice. "Before the cuckoo clock strikes ten tonight, he will be gone, so gone," and the phone went dead.

"That bastard, the no good bastard," she cried. "It's Conrad. I know it's him," and her heart started racing. Her nerves were suddenly jumping out of her skin, and she was perspiring. She started pacing, boiling with anger and feeling totally helpless.

"My, God, Ed," she suddenly cried out. The call is referring to him," and the realization he was out, and vulnerable to danger gave her a sick feeling in her stomach. "Please God, don't let any harm come to him," and her words were frantic. "Please," she begged, and she started to sob.

The unpleasant recollection of the last series of phone calls she had received suddenly cluttered her mind. They had mushroomed into a conspiracy that almost destroyed her physically and emotionally. The thought of another horrible incident made her more frantic.

"I can't take much more of this," she wailed. This time she feared Ed was in danger. She walked over to the window and pressed her forehead against the glass, her hands cupped against the sides of her face as she looked out hoping to get a glimpse of him.

As she waited impatiently, Ed left the convenience store with the matches and walked briskly to the car, in a hurry to get back to an anxious Abigail. Once he was inside the car, a figure with a nylon stocking over his head rose from behind his seat and placed the barrel of a nine millimeter hand gun against the back of his head.

"Christ," he blurted in surprise. "What's going on?" and fear gripped him.

"Don't say a word and listen," and the intruder pushed the barrel with more force against him. "You're going to drive your car by that pay phone," and he pointed to one by the rear side of the building. "Then you're going to get out and call her."

"Call who?"

"Don't play stupid with me," said the intruder, and he thumped Ed on the head with the stock of the gun. "The one you're staying with. Now, I don't want to hear another word unless I ask."

Ed's mind was racing. Who was this man? Who was behind him? Why did he want him to call Abigail? How could he get away from him, and was his life in danger? There were so many unanswered questions, and his fears were intensifying.

"Now drive the car to the phone," the intruder commanded. "And drive it slowly. If you try anything foolish, I'll kill you on the spot and the girl later. This gun is equipped with a silencer. You're not dealing with some punk amateur," and not for a moment did Ed doubt him.

The car was at the phone. "Now, get out and dial, and then stand by the window so I can hear your conversation. You're going to tell her you can't see her anymore, and you will be leaving Connecticut immediately and permanently once you hang up the phone. No further explanation will be necessary," and his voice was as cold as ice. "If you don't leave or try to contact her again, she will be killed."

Ed suddenly felt sick. My God, he thought. This will inevitably destroy Abigail, and she won't know why it all happened. His stomach was sour, and he felt like he was going to vomit.

"I repeat, don't try anything foolish, like dialing 911 or trying to run. If I don't call in that everything went well, the girl will die. She won't be able to hide. She'll always be looking over her shoulder and living in fear. If you really love her, you will permanently stay far away from her," and the intruder pushed the gun hard into his neck. "Do you understand me?"

"Yes, I do," and they were the most difficult words he ever had to speak in his life. It was clear now. Someone wanted to keep him permanently away from Abigail, and there was only one person who came into his mind. It was Conrad. How could he become so bitter and hateful? They had been friends, for God sake. How could he now be so desperate and unforgiving? And now be capable enough to commit an unspeakable, heinous crime to complete his act of vengeance.

Ed was distraught. He was dying a thousand deaths thinking about giving up his love for Abigail to save her life. He would do it. He loved her too much to take the chance if the intruder was really serious about killing her. He prayed God would give her the strength to accept it and go on with her life.

He got out of the car and did as the intruder asked. He dialed the phone, and when he heard her say hello he knew something was wrong. "Abigail, this is Ed."

"Ed, where are you?" she asked, her voice stressed. "I had another one of those phone calls. I think you're in danger. Please come home now," and she was speaking rapidly. He was dying inside as she spoke, his heart in agony, shattering into a thousand pieces.

He tried to speak, but his throat was tightening, and he felt like he was going to choke to death.

"Ed, are you there?" and there was panic in her voice. "Ed, talk to me."

His heart palpated momentarily, and it made him cough. "Abigail," the words wisped from his throat. I… I can't see you anymore," and the words were spoken weakly.

"What! What did you say? You can't see me anymore?" and her voice was hysterical. "What are you saying? Don't do this to me. Please don't do this," and she was crying.

His eyes started to tear as he listened to her. How he wanted to tell her the truth. Perhaps the intruder was hired to only frighten him. Perhaps Conrad was bluffing if it indeed was him. But if the threat was real, and he attempted to thwart it in anyway and Abigail was killed, he would be as responsible as if he pulled the trigger himself.

"Is somebody there with you? Is someone threatening you?" Abigail asked desperately seeking answers for what was happening.

The intruder now signaled him to terminate the conversation.

"I love you, Abigail," he desperately wanted to assure her, and before she could say another word he hung up. He wished he could have held her one more time before leaving.

The gunman signaled him to come to the car. "You did well. Get in and listen. If you ever make contact with her again, she will die. You both will be watched. You are to go to California and stay there. When I get out of the car, start driving and don't look back."

Ed nodded, and he felt like he had slipped into the inferno of hell. It was the lowest moment of his existence. He started the car, and as he left the parking area he didn't look back.

Ed was reluctantly driving his car in a westerly direction as Abigail was wiping the tears from her cheeks. She was crying uncontrollably, pacing and lamenting out loud. "What have they done to the man I love. Oh, God, why won't you help us?" and she didn't understand why so many terrible things were happening in her life. "I need a drink. I need a drink," she repeated. She quickly poured some run over ice in a glass and started drinking it. When she finished it she poured herself another, and she wasted no time putting it down. Moments later the affect of the alcohol began to relax her.

She was able to think a little more clearly. "Ed loves me too much. He wouldn't leave me she tried to reason. That bastard Conrad threatened him. He wants to break us up," she said to herself totally convinced. Then she started to laugh cynically, and with remorse said, "The bastard already has."

Her eyes started tearing. "I need a drink," and she poured still another. She drank it quickly, and a short time later she passed out.

It was eleven the next morning when Abigail opened her eyes. She was on the couch unaware as to how she had gotten there. She felt like hell had swarmed over her. Her head was aching and throbbing, and her stomach was sour.

After sitting up for a moment, the horrible memories of the night before came back and started to haunt her. They were to make love when Ed came back from the store. Instead he never returned. Something horrible had to have happened to make him call with the nerve-shattering message he couldn't see her again breaching the short period of their reconciliation. And not knowing exactly what it was added to her grief. She was now entrenched with the dismal realization Ed was gone, truly gone, and there really wasn't a damn thing she could do. Then again, maybe there was something she could do. She could go to the police. Yes, they would help her once they heard what she had to say.

She quickly tried to get cleaned up although her body wasn't capable of reacting as quickly as she would have liked. Later, she was satisfied she looked reasonably respectable to make an appearance at the police station.

Once at the police station, the first person she approached was a sergeant Carter. "I want to report a missing person. "My boyfriend Ed, to be specific," she informed him.

"And your name, maim?"

"Abigail Mc Cloud," she quickly responded.

"And your address?" the sergeant asked.

"Can I give you all this kind of information later? My boyfriend is missing, and that's more important right now," and she was becoming impatient.

"We'll get to your boyfriend in a minute. First, I need you to cooperate and provide me with some information."

She would do as the sergeant requested. She did need the help of the police. When the sergeant was finished with his questions he asked, "How long has your boyfriend been missing?"

"Since last night," she quickly informed him.

The sergeant raised his eyebrows and said, "Since last night? A person has to be missing forty eight hours before they are considered officially missing. I'm sorry I can't help you now."

"That's bull shit," Abigail said with distinct anger ringing in her voice. "Someone abducted or threatened him last night. He would never leave me. I just know it."

"How was your relationship when you last saw him?"

"Fine," she snapped. "We were going to make love. Then he decided to go to the convenience store and get some candles. Does that sound like a guy who was interested in leaving me?" and she looked sternly into the sergeant's eyes.

"I guess not," the sergeant reasoned.

"There is one more thing of significance I have to mention," said Abigail. "He called me from the store. By the sound of his voice, I knew something was wrong, very wrong," and her facial expression was stressed. "He said he couldn't see me anymore and that he loved me. There wasn't anymore conversation, and he never came back," and she started to sob.

"I see," said the sergeant. "If he doesn't show or you don't hear from him in the next thirty eight hours we'll file a missing person report. That's all I can do right now."

Abigail looked down and then looked at the sergeant with disappointment. "So that's it?" she said softly suddenly feeling helpless. "Thank you, sergeant," and she left the police station.

Two days later, Abigail was back at the police station to speak to Sergeant Carter. "I haven't heard from my boyfriend Ed."

"Okay, I'll file the missing person report."

"Then what?" she was quick to ask.

"We'll send a detective to investigate the area you last heard from him. More likely than not it would be in the vicinity of the convenience store you mentioned."

"Please let me know what you find out. You have my phone number."

When no information turned up on Ed two weeks later, Abigail was convinced she would never see him again. She couldn't focus on anything but what could have happened to him. She hadn't eaten very much, and it was safe to say most of her body fluid came from the consumption of alcohol. She had not made an appearance at her place of employment since Ed's disappearance.

She was totally confused how she could feel such a strong love for Ed in such a short period of time, especially after having a relationship with Conrad just a few months before. But she couldn't deny her true feelings. And she couldn't deny her intuition. An intuition that remembered the horrible words of the phone call that said the devil would take him away. With pain, she was convinced Ed was gone, and gone for good.

It made her feel a terrible emptiness deep inside. Life had gone bad, and all the purpose and meaning were now gone. She couldn't take any more pain and disappointment. The thought of not seeing Ed again was unbearable. Unmistakably, Conrad was evil and the devil in her life, and she was now a slave to it. No, she wouldn't let him destroy her and give him the honor and satisfaction. She would take her own life, willingly. She, Abigail Theresa McCloud would now give back the gift of life she no longer valued. Without hesitation she walked into the bathroom and took a razor from the cabinet. The mirror above the vanity reflected her image, sullen, distraught, the white of her eyes badly bloodshot. Then, in a moment of despair and weakness, she calmly sliced the skin on her wrists with the razor, and crimson drops of blood dripped into the sink.

CHAPTER 17

"Wake up, Abigail. Don't you die on me," Barbara Willis was saying forcefully. "Come on, Abigail, wake up."

Roy Bellows had wrapped both of Abigail's wrists tightly with clean face cloths to help stop the bleeding. "Where's the bloody ambulance?" he moaned impatient for its arrival.

Barbara again nudged Abigail by the shoulders determined to get her to open her eyes. Then she slapped her cheeks lightly in an attempt to stimulate her.

In the distance a siren was screaming, and Roy heard it first. "Finally, the bloody ambulance is coming," and he walked rapidly to the window. He could see the blinking red lights as the vehicle streaked toward the building.

"Her eyes are open," Barbara shouted from the bathroom feeling some relief. "Abigail, you're going to be okay. Talk to me, honey."

She saw Barbara's face, and the image was a blur. Then it faded before her as her eyes closed. A moment later they again opened.

"Ed's gone," she slurred, with her words barely audible.

"Don't worry about anything right now," Barbara tried to comfort her. "Help is on the way."

Abigail heard the sound of a siren, and then it stopped. A moment later she saw two men hurriedly enter the bathroom and come toward her. Seconds later her eyes closed and she lost consciousness.

When Abigail's eyes opened again, she was in the hospital. An intravenous unit was hooked up to her arm, and her wrists were bandaged. Barbara and Roy were sitting by her bedside.

"Welcome back, Abigail," said Barbara. "You gave us both a scare."

"You're going to be fine, yes indeed," Roy was happy to inform her.

She looked at them and her eyes started to tear. "I'm sorry," she apologized. "Ed is gone. I'm so upset."

Barbara took hold of her hand and squeezed it. "Don't talk about it now. You need to get your strength back. You rest now. Roy and I are going to leave for a while. We'll be back later. When you feel better, we'll talk about it." Barbara kissed her on the forehead first, and then Roy. "We love you, honey," Barbara said with emotion.

"I love you, too," Abigail said softly, and after they left she closed her eyes.

Conrad was standing by the railing on the balcony of his condo, savoring the sight of the rising sun. It appeared like a large, orange colored coined dollar sliced in half, the bottom half still shielded by the curvature of the earth.

He felt good, ready to greet the new day. After receiving the brief phone message that had said, "It's done," Conrad felt revitalized with a feeling of closure. Yes, the closure he so desperately needed. Maybe now his vengeance with Abigail could finally be put to rest.

Perhaps it was his insecurity that surfaced at times, but he had to be certain on such an important matter that Ed's departure wasn't just a temporary thing. He had to be certain even though it meant making a trip to the Lechner Apartment complex to see if there was any sign of Ed's presence or his car.

Later in the morning after showering and eating breakfast, Conrad parked his car in the lot of the Lechner Apartment complex. He walked around casually searching for Ed's car. To his satisfaction there was no sign of it.

When he started back to his car a young man was walking toward him. As he approached Conrad he said, "Did you hear the commotion here yesterday morning?"

"No, I didn't," Conrad answered figuring the stranger thought he lived there.

"Oh, yes, an ambulance and fire truck arrived around eleven in the morning."

"What happened?" Conrad asked out of curiosity.

"Some young girl was brought out on a stretcher. I could see blood on the bandages around her wrists. Rumors are she tried to commit suicide. But who knows. You know how rumors are."

Conrad gave him a delayed response, his mind suddenly preoccupied with Abigail. "Yes, I know," he answered.

"Catch you later," said the stranger, and he went into the building with Conrad watching him.

"Christ, I wonder if it was Abigail," he said aloud. Then he realized that for a passing moment he was concerned. "Why should I care if it was?" he said to himself. No, he wouldn't permit himself to care.

Later in the afternoon, he pulled his car onto the parking apron of a three story, office building constructed in the early sixties. The exterior of the building was in need of refurbishing, and the structure was rented primarily by small businesses, various professionals and service agencies.

Conrad was standing in front of a raised panel, oak door with a plate that read SAMUAL BOWERS—PRIVATE INVESTIGATOR. He knocked on the door and entered a small reception area furnished with a few chairs and a small table with some non-current magazines scattered on the surface. A four-foot, high counter separated the reception area from an adjoining office. A moment later a tall, lanky man with graying hair and mustache greeted him.

"Samuel Bowers, he introduced himself. How can I help you?"

"I'm Conrad Hill, and I believe I can use your services."

"That's what I'm here for. What can I do for you?" he asked blinking his eyes frequently.

"I need to have an individual placed under surveillance twenty four hours a day until further notice. Are you able to do that?"

"Let's go into my office," and Conrad followed him. "Have a seat," and there were two, old wooden chairs with arm rests placed in front of an oak desk. Conrad seated himself and Samuel took a folder out of a drawer from a metal file cabinet and dropped it on the desk before he sat down. He rested both his arms on the desk and studied Conrad for a moment, blinking his eyes excessively.

"Who's the person you want placed under surveillance?"

"It's a girl from the area. Her name is Abigail McCloud."

"What's her address?" Samuel asked without looking up.

"She rents in the Lechner Apartment complex, unit 101-A. The building is at 2083 Bennett Place."

"What's the relationship?" and he looked at Conrad.

"Does it matter?" and he preferred he didn't have to know.

Samuel blinked his eyes and sat back in his chair. Then he tapped the pen in his grasp on the desk. "I like to know the facts when I take on a case. It gives me a better feel for what I'm doing. Don't worry. What I do for you is confidential. Will you work with me or not?"

Conrad thought about it for a moment. Perhaps he was right. Maybe he would do a better job. He did say the information he needed would be confidential. "Okay, I'll give you all the information you need."

"Good, you're paying the bill. So let me do my job. What's your relationship with the girl?"

"She's my ex-girlfriend," and he hated saying it.

"How is your relationship now?"

Conrad hesitated for a moment. Did he really have to know everything? "I haven't seen her in over a month," he decided to tell him. "The only thing I'm sure about is that she's dating someone."

"How did you come across that bit of information?" and Samuel was curious.

"I saw her at one of the local restaurants. So I'm assuming she's dating."

"I see," and his eyes were blinking again. "So, tell me exactly what you want me to do for you, Mr. Hill."

Conrad moistened his lips. "I want you to tell me what she does from the time she gets up until the time she goes to bed. I'd like to get a status report weekly. Can you manage that?"

"I can arrange it. My fee is two hundred a day plus expenses, with a five hundred dollar advance. And there is no room for negotiation. It's up to you Mr. Hill. For your peace of mind, I've handled several similar cases. There are all kinds of people out there who have sought my services. I haven't let anyone down yet, but sometimes my findings are more disturbing than expected. Get my drift?" he said trying to make him cognizant of the possibility of having regrets later.

"Thank you for your concern, Mr. Bowers. The case is yours," and Conrad shook his hand and wrote him a check in the amount of the advance, and Conrad thought, How the hell can he see anything with his eyes blinking like that?

Three days later Conrad received a call from Samuel Bowers. "I have some information for you. Can you come down to my office this afternoon, between two and four?"

"I'll be there," Conrad said with eagerness in his voice. He couldn't help but wonder what information Samuel had uncovered, and he was at the office by two fifteen.

"You're probably wondering why I called you before the week was up," Samuel started the conversation.

"The thought did cross my mind," and it made Conrad think the Blinking Man, the nickname he gave him, hit on something important.

Samuel blinked his eyes excessively and said, "Truth is there was no activity from her apartment for the first two days. Her car never moved from the parking space, and no lights were lit in the apartment. So my investigation went in a different direction." He opened a desk drawer and handed Conrad a large envelope. "Go ahead, open it," and Samuel sat back in his chair.

Conrad opened it and pulled out a picture of a building with a large, concrete marquee on the lawn that read PHILMORE PHYSIACTRIC HOSPITAL.

"What's this?" he asked with a puzzled, facial expression.

"Your ex-girlfriend Abigail was admitted there earlier in the week. She attempted suicide," he said blinking. "I don't think she is going anywhere for a while."

"How were you able to get this information so soon?" Conrad asked, surprised and pleased.

"It's my job. It's your job to trust me and pay the bills. Simple as that," Samuel said calmly.

Samuel doesn't miss much for a guy who blinks so much, Conrad thought.

The picture made Conrad think, the stranger in the parking lot was talking about Abigail. I guess I got her good this time. And he remembered what he had said to her the day he went to her office and informed her about the conspiracy he and Ed had executed. "Vengeance is mine, sayeth Conrad." He broke into laughter and Samuel looked on blinking his eyes.

Yes, he had gotten her good. And obviously, Ed was out of her life. He had gotten him too, and it felt good to know that Ed, his no good bastard friend paid a heavy price for his perfidious behavior that breached their friendship. What did he expect? Conrad had reasoned, a reward for betrayal? And as Conrad thought about it, appearing to be oblivious to Samuel's presence, he laughed again like a joyous conqueror enveloped in the ecstasy of vengeance.

Perhaps he could now place Abigail on a shelf of the past and concentrate on his next victims, Penny and Erica. Oh yes, there had to be more victims. Vengeance was sweet, and he liked the way it tasted.

Conrad slid the picture back into the envelope. Then he looked at Samuel who had been studying him. "I guess I won't need your services any longer, Mr. Bowers. You did well, and if I ever have a need I'll certainly give you a call. If you can tell me what I owe you, I'll write you a check now."

"I'd appreciate that, Mr. Hill. I have a detailed account right here," and he removed a document from a folder on his desk. Conrad studied it for a moment, and then wrote a check.

As he left the office, he immediately thought of Penny, and a smile flitted across his lips.

CHAPTER 18

Conrad was eager to continue grooming Penny Hennessey for the big fall. He had been temporarily diverted from seeing her when Abigail had unexpectedly forgiven Ed for conspiring against her. He had lost some time, but the pain and agony Abigail had finally sustained more than made up for it.

Now he was free to pursue Penny and make her emotions a slave to his desires. He would derive great satisfaction from exploiting her vulnerability. On the other hand, the homely, little bitch would benefit from being lavished with attention, affection and the promise of a dream relationship while it lasted.

At six in the evening Conrad was on the phone with Penny. "How you doing?" he asked with enthusiasm.

"Okay, I guess."

"I didn't forget you. It's important that you know that. I've been busy taking care of a matter that confronted me unexpectedly. I hope you didn't think I forgot about you," he deliberately repeated to convince her of his concern.

"I wasn't thinking that. I thought you might call," she said, though she was uncertain if he would.

"Absolutely I would. I enjoyed your company the last time we were together. How would you like to go out this Saturday? I thought I could take you to the casino at the Indian reservation in Foxwood," he informed her before she could answer his question concerning her willingness to go out Saturday. "Would you like that?"

She hesitated a moment. She had never been to a casino. Money was always tight. Some of the girls at work had gone and loved it. A few had even won some money. Now he was asking to take her.

"I'd love to go, but I'm afraid I'm naive when it comes to gambling. You will have to show me what to do."

"No problem. It's a piece of cake. You know what they say. Beginners have luck."

She laughed. "Oh yes, I'm a beginner all right."

"You will be fine. We're going to need a jumpstart on the evening. It's a busy place, so why don't I pick you up at five o'clock. Tell your mom it will be a late evening so she won't be worried, and that I'll take good care of you."

"Okay, I'll go with you," and she was excited.

"Very good, and I'll see you Saturday at five."

When Penny hung up the phone she placed her hand over her heart. "Wow, I'm going to the casino. I'll have to let the girls at work know. And with a handsome guy; what will they think about that?" and she smiled, eager for Saturday to arrive.

Penny's parents were pleased to see how excited she was when Saturday arrived. Both her parents were on disability and knew how much of their daughter's time was spent caring for them and handling household affairs. They were well aware of the many sacrifices she had made in their behalf. They also knew how introverted she was, and how it caused her to go long periods of time without any social life. It went without saying they were pleased and grateful Conrad was again taking their daughter out on a date.

When Conrad called on Penny, her parents made sure they were in the living room so they could greet him.

"Nice to see you again, Mr. Hill," Penny's mother spoke first.

"Pleased to meet you, sir," Mr. Hennessey said, for he hadn't been present when Conrad had taken Penny out the first time.

"I'm pleased to meet you, Mr. Hennessey," and Conrad shook his hand. Then he turned his attention to Penny who was wearing a black dress, black high heal shoes, and a white pearl necklace. "You look lovely, Penny," said Conrad, and the compliment pleased her parents as much as it pleased her.

"Thank, you," she said shyly.

Then Conrad asked, "Are you ready to leave?"

"Yes, I'm ready," and she raised her eyebrows.

"Don't worry, I'll take good care of her," Conrad said to her parents.

"We know you will," her mother said. And when they left she turned to her husband and said, "He is such a fine, young man."

"Yes, dear, he appears to be," Mr. Hennessey commented.

Once they were on the road headed for Foxwood, Penny said, "I always wanted a Trans-Am. I love their style," and her eyes roamed over the interior of the car.

"Perhaps you'll hit it big at the casino. A lot of times people like you who don't know the ins and outs of gambling win big," and he looked at her and smiled encouragingly.

"I don't think so. I don't mean to sound like a pessimist, but I never had much in the form of luck. Besides, I don't have very much money with me."

"I don't want you to even think about that. You're my date, remember? I'll take care of all our needs. I want you to have a good time, Penny."

She was silent, consumed by his generosity. She wasn't looking for any handout. Her life had never been materialistic due to her family circumstances. And she had learned early in life not to expect too much. However, she did greatly appreciate when someone did something for her, especially in a gracious manner.

"I thank you for taking me out tonight, Conrad," she finally spoke after a brief moment of silence. "My life has been terribly dull," she confessed.

"Well, it's going to start changing for the better. That's a promise," and he placed his hand on hers momentarily and squeezed it.

The unexpected gesture made her inhale quickly, and not knowing how to react she felt awkward. Yet, she was pleased it happened. It felt good to feel him, and she could only construe it was an outward manifestation of his growing feelings for her. Feelings she welcomed and yet confused her. From what she had seen of him he was handsome, generous, kind and considerate. What girl wouldn't like those qualities? And as painful as it was, she admittedly didn't understand why he wasn't pursuing a relationship with some beautiful, voluptuous female.

Penny focused her attention on the road ahead of her. They were on a one-lane road following a trailer truck, and Conrad was growing impatient following it. "Watch this, Penny," and he nudged her arm. "I'm going to blow this pain in the ass away."

There was a small stretch of road that was clear, and Conrad flipped his signal light on. He pulled out starting to accelerate when the trailer truck moved to the left almost hitting his right, front fender thwarting his attempt to pass.

"That freaking scumbag," Conrad blurted. "What the hell is he trying to do?"

The incident made Penny nervous, and her hands gripped forcefully the sides of the seat. She looked at Conrad, silently pleading with her eyes for him to be careful.

"Next chance I get I'm passing the low life. A lot of these truck drivers are homicidal maniacs," he said livid with anger. "Teach him not to screw around with me."

Penny sat back in her seat and nervously tugged on the seat belt to make sure it was snug.

"Don't worry, I'm not going to put us in jeopardy," Conrad tried to assure her. "You did say you always wanted to own a Trans-Am. I'll show you in a minute what this baby is capable of doing."

Conrad leaned left to see if the passing lane had a clear space. There was a car in the distance he felt he could beat. Without warning he pulled out slamming the accelerator to the floor. The engine roared and Penny felt her back press against the seat from the forward thrust of the car.

The truck started to move to the left but the Trans-Am streaked by before it posed a threat. "Take that, you low life bastard," and Conrad said it with rancor. Then he laughed with a high pitch of emotion as he watched the truck in the rear view mirror fall further behind. "Choke on my dust, you scumbag."

It was the second time Penny had seen him put on an exhibition of anger and hatred. The incident at the parking lot where she hit his care and Conrads harsh words were still freshly embedded in her mind. But she really couldn't fault him this time. The truck— and for no apparent reason—could have caused them to have a serious accident.

Conrad, much calmer, looked at her and smiled. "Want to drive?"

"No, thank you. I don't think I could have handled that truck. I think I have to learn gradually how to handle one of these cars at high speed," and her insecurity was obvious to Conrad.

"One of these days I'll put you behind the wheel. You'll do just fine. Trust me, okay?"

"I do," she said, and unbeknownst to her the word trust would take on a new definition.

When they arrived at the Foxwood Pequot Indian reservation, Penny found the sight awesome. She had no predetermined notion or vision as to what to expect. The structure that housed five casinos and the nearby towering hotel were a beautiful sight to see. She found the atmosphere electrifying and became excited. She took hold of Conrad's arm and said, "I love it. Thank you so much for bringing me here."

"We can come anytime you wish," he promised her. "Penny want a casino?" he joked.

"I get it," she said after realizing what he was referring to. She was even more impressed when they went inside. There were people everywhere, and it reminded her of a busy shopping mall. There were stores, eating establishments, eye catching décor along the walkways, and of course the gaming rooms with their strange sounds of coins, beeps, bells, and voices expressing pleasure and disappointment.

"Let's get you into one of these gaming rooms for some action. Then we can get something to eat. Sound okay?"

"Anything you say," and her eyes were roaming taking in the sights as she spoke.

"That's fine," and he took her by the hand. "I'm going to give you two hundred dollars to play the slot machines. I'll give you some pointers on what the machines are capable of doing, and then you play whatever you desire. Just don't leave your place if lights flash on a pole above your machine and sounds go off. It could mean big money."

"Okay," and she was as excited as a child on Christmas morning looking at gifts Santa left under the tree during the night.

After Conrad briefed her and got change, he said, "Stay in the general area so we don't become separated. Otherwise, I might lose you. I'll be back later to check on you. Good Luck, Penny," and she smiled at him excitedly.

She found the machines easy to play, not complicated as she had imagined. She particularly liked pulling the handle as opposed to using the electronic buttons. When Penny experienced her first payout, she felt embarrassed and looked around to see if anyone was watching her. But no one seemed to care to her surprise. They were obviously focused on their own expectations of hitting the jackpot.

A time later Conrad returned to Penny. "How's it going?"

"Okay, but I did lose thirty dollars," and she felt a little guilty since it was his money.

"Don't worry about it, Penny. There's more where that came from. Want to take a break and get some food?" he asked.

"Sure, anything you say."

He thought a moment. "I think I'll take you to the buffet so that you can have a chance to experience some different types of food. The restaurant offers food representative of five different areas of the world, and he took her by the hand. He had no idea how much it pleased her.

Penny enjoyed the buffet immensely, and it was another impressive moment of her experience at the casino.

When they were finished eating, Conrad took her to see the large statue of the Pequot Indian. It was positioned atop a waterfall, surrounded by sculptured deer, rocks and vegetation. The scene was embellished with strategic lighting with the re-enactment of a thunderstorm.

Penny thought it conveyed serenity, peace, the beauty of nature, and then sadness. Sadness because the American Indian eventually lost everything the scene depicted.

"I can't say enough about the beauty of this place," she said. "Everyone should have the opportunity to see it," and she thought about her parents. "Next time I come I'm going to bring my camera so I can take pictures so that my parents can see this amazing place."

Conrad studied her for a moment. "Hell, Penny, we can take them here. We'll manage."

"You mean you would do that for them?" and she was both surprised and over whelmed.

"Of course I would," making it sound like it was no big deal.

"But you hardly know them," and her amazement persisted.

"I know you, don't I?" and he placed his arm around her.

Her eyes started to tear. "You are the kindest person. You have no idea how much I appreciate your offer to bring my parents here."

"Just tell me when. Come on, let's get back to the machines and win some money."

This time Conrad sat her down at a dollar machine and gave her one hundred dollars in coins. "You can play this one a hundred times or double up on your bets and play less. Just let your spirit move you and have fun. I'll be back to see how you're doing."

"Thank you, Conrad," and with a smile of gratitude she watched him walk away.

While Penny played the dollar slot machine, Conrad tried his luck at the crap table. After a few roles, a stunning, attractive blond in her early twenties took a place next to him. She was dressed in a low cut, red dress with a hemline well above the knees that accentuated her sexuality. Almost immediately she said, "Any luck?"

Conrad smiled and answered, "Not yet."

"Maybe I'll give you some," and she placed some chips next to his on the pass line. A new roller threw the dice and when they came to a halt the croupier shouted, "And it's seven."

Conrad was pleased. It was the first time he won at the table. He turned and faced the blonde. "Does lady luck have a name?"

"I'm Roxanne," and she placed some chips on the hard eight with Conrad following suit after she nodded for him to play the same.

The roller threw the dice again making them bounce off the sidewall of the table, and when they came to rest each dice read the number four. "And it's eight, hard," the croupier called out.

Conrad couldn't believe he had won again. Who was this girl who had the intuition to win every time she played? Or did she posses some mystical, physic power?

"Your name, handsome?" she asked placing her mouth close to his ear.

"Conrad, Ms. Luck."

"Here, play the number twelve on the field," she said softly, and he quickly placed some chips next to hers. She can't win again, he thought, and he anxiously waited for the roll of the dice. The roller threw the dice and they stopped displaying the number twelve.

"My, God," he mumbled softly. "You picked another winner. How do you do it?" he had to ask.

"My secret, handsome, and I'm not telling. I can tell you something else," and she took him by the arm and led him a short distance away from the table.

"And what may that be?" his curiosity increasing by the second.

She looked at him seductively. "You are dying to go to bed with me."

She was right. When he first saw her in the red dress he was aroused sexually, and his first thought was going to bed with her. He didn't deny it. "Unfortunately, I'm with someone," he said with regret. "Perhaps you can give me your phone number."

She opened her purse and gave him a card. "Call me, you won't be sorry," and she stepped forward and gave him a kiss on the lips.

She smiled, and when he turned to watch her walk away he noticed Penny standing in the direction in which Roxanne was headed.

She certainly must have observed the kiss, was Conrad's first thought. And from the look on Penny's face, she had. She wasted no time approaching Conrad. "What was that all about?" and she surprised herself with her aggressiveness.

He hesitated for a moment. "Ugh, I rolled the dice well and as a result she won some money. She kind of rewarded me with a kiss. It was totally innocent." He had to keep her happy, but deep inside he resented the homely, little bitch questioning him.

"What made you leave your machine?" he asked.

"I won eight hundred dollars," she said excitedly.

"That's wonderful, Penny. I'm happy for you."

He was happy for her, and when she won, she couldn't wait to tell him. Then she realized that winning suddenly hadn't mattered when she saw the blonde kissing him. Instead, she had become concerned and upset, and obviously cared a great deal about him to make her momentarily put the excitement of winning aside. Yes, in a fraction the strange blonde made her experience the fear of losing him, a treasure in her eyes so early in their relationship. It was a horrible feeling, and she hoped she would never experience it again.

His explanation about the kiss pacified her. After all, it was possible. The evening was wonderful, and she wanted to keep it that way.

"Come on," Conrad said. "Let's go play some slots."

"Okay, but first I want to give you your money back," said Penny.

"No, No, you keep it."

"But I won. You deserve to get it back," she insisted. "You were so kind to give it to me."

"I'm happy you won, and I want you to keep it. Take your parents out to dinner. I won't change my mind," and he took hold of her hand and led her to the dollar slots.

At midnight they left the casino.

After Conrad pulled his Trans-Am up to the curb and parked in front of Penny's house she said, "I had the most wonderful time, Conrad."

"I'm glad, and so did I. I want you to know that I have strong feelings for you, Penny. I want to date you steady if that's okay with you."

She slid to the edge of her seat and leaned over and hugged him. She was beaming with happiness. "I feel the same way." She studied him for a moment. "Actually, tonight has convinced me God sent you to me. Now I know why I backed into your car. I feel totally different about life since you and I met each other," and she looked away shyly.

"If He did, I'm glad. I think you're a great girl," and he kissed her long and with passion. "Good night, Penny."

When he left she realized she was already in love with him. It made her reaffirm her belief that God had sent him. Yes, he had been sent, not by God, but by the devil.

CHAPTER 19

"Hi, Conrad, and how have you been?" asked Charlene Lavoie, the receptionist at the

Hill Development Corporation.

"I'm okay, and yourself?"

"Fine, thank you. Here to see your dad?"

"Yes, I am. Nice seeing you again, Charlene," and he headed for his father's office.

Charlene was sincerely happy to see Conrad. Actually, she harbored a crush on him that had persisted ever since she became employed at his father's business over a year ago.

Charlene stood five feet tall, possessed an attractive face with impeccable clear skin, and had bright, brown eyes. Her body was well proportioned, and by Conrad's descriptive standards, had a beautiful, little ass. She was also incredibly large busted, and it went without saying her breasts were the focal point of numerous male visitors to the lobby. Charlene's personality was quite fitting for her position as receptionist, amiable, loquacious and fastidious when it came to her personal appearance. But she didn't believe in being aggressive with men when it came to making new acquaintances. She had the old school attitude that men should be the pursuers of women if they were interested in developing a relationship.

Prior to Conrad's leave of absence, she and Conrad had conversed often and were frequent lunch companions. Charlene had hoped the lunches would turn into dinner engagements, then dates and a rewarding relationship. Even though it had not yet happened, she had not given up hope that such a possibility would materialize.

When Conrad approached his father's secretary Rhonda, he already knew what his father was going to say. Surely he was going to address his leave of absence. So what's the big deal missing some time, thought Conrad. Hill Development Corporation was doing fine without him. His father had other engineers in his employ. If they weren't good enough to calculate hydraulics and drainage properly they should be replaced with more competent personnel. A company shouldn't have to depend so heavily on any one individual such as himself. And that was exactly how he felt.

"Your father's expecting you, Conrad," said Rhonda breaking his concentration.

He hadn't seen his father in three weeks and it hadn't bothered him. Subconsciously, he was avoiding both his parents because he disliked being lectured. Ever since his breakup with Abigail they had found his lack of ability to adjust to the situation unacceptable. To Conrad, it appeared they where holding him in contempt.

When Conrad entered the office, his father spoke first. "Sit down, son." Mr. Hill ran his fingers across his chin while studying his son. "I need you here at work. The Bakersfield Mall project is progressing well and is ready for the storm frequency calculation along with the area drainage. I don't want the project held up. I think your leave of absence has been over-extended. Furthermore, I think I've been more than generous," and he waited for some response.

Conrad shifted his body in the chair indicative of his nervousness. "I've had a hard time adjusting to the loss of Abigail. I don't think you and mother understand. You're being totally unsympathetic. I need more time," he pleaded.

"That's bull shit, Conrad. Do you want to know what I really think?"

"Sure, give your godly, fathomed opinion, father. You're so damn omniscient."

"I think you enjoy wallowing in your self pity not doing anything responsible and living off your grandfather's trust fund. Abigail isn't the only female available in the world. Give someone else a chance. You have a lot going for you," and he stood up and looked out the large window behind his desk. Then he turned and faced Conrad. "Must I remind you of the terms of your trust? Your grandfather specified you could draw money as long as you remained employed and conducted yourself in a responsible manner. Otherwise you would default, and I as acting fiduciary would have no alternative but to freeze your trust."

"Is that a threat, father?" he snapped, totally indignant.

"Call it what you will, but I do expect you to be at work tomorrow. Do I make myself clear?"

He loathed him. Yes, he loathed his father, at least for the moment. "Are you finished?" Conrad asked with bitterness.

"I think I made myself clear. It's your call, son."

"I'm out of here," he said with an expression of disgust, and when he left he slammed the office door. When he walked by Rhonda she heard him say, "The no good bastard."

When Conrad returned to his condo, he made himself a drink. Then he sat in the armchair by the fireplace. He had to think. His father had placed a large obstacle in his path. And this obstacle conveyed a connotation of blackmail. He felt like he was being choked, and he resented it. If he didn't work, he would be cut off financially. It was as simple as that.

"The bastard is blackmailing me," he lamented. "It's freaking blackmail," he repeated. His father's alternative gave him no choice but to return to work. He needed the money to carry out his plans for Penny and Erica. To his dismay he didn't have to think long about it. He would capitulate to his father, as repugnant as it would be, the only consolation being it would enable him to complete his mission of revenge.

Hatred had taken over his life, and it seemed there was little room for anything else. Conrad's first thought was to retaliate against his father. He could very conveniently screw up his storm frequency and drainage calculations for the Bakersfield Mall. It would hurt his father badly and cause serious repercussions when the area became flooded or had serious drainage problems every time there was excessive rainfall. And how would they be able to prove he did it deliberately? After all, it could be an honest oversight. Figures could inadvertently be miscalculated and not readily discernable. Oh, how enticing the thought was. He would definitely give it serious consideration. And Conrad thought, Vengeance shall be mine, sayeth Conrad.

He got up from the armchair and made himself another drink. Then he paced for a moment with the drink in his hand. The argument with his father had stirred up the venom of hate in his veins. It made his mind zero in on Erica and Penny now that he had a tentative plan of revenge for the Hill Development Corporation.

Conrad again seated himself in the armchair. He could think the best when he was comfortable and able to lean on the crutch of alcohol. He rested his head on the back cushion and closed his eyes, thinking, plotting and scheming. A while later, he smiled and said, "Yes, it should work."

He would call Erica and keep her involved with him. She had enjoyed his company immensely the last time they were together. Yes, he would keep her involved. After spending a day with her he would go back to Penny. Since he was winning her over more quickly than he had anticipated, he would accelerate his plans. The sooner she fell the sooner he would taste the sweet wine of vengeance.

Conrad had thought enough. Now it was time to relax. The meeting with his father had been stressful. The stress and the relaxing affect of the alcohol made him drowsy and his eyes closed. As he started to slip into slumber he murmured, "Abigail, why did you leave me?"

Conrad had Erica on the phone. "How would you like to do some sight seeing?" he asked.

"Sure, I enjoy doing that. What did you have in mind?"

"The two of us observing the Lockwood-Mathews Mansion that was utilized sparingly in the movie, THE STEPFORD WIVES," he informed her. It was built in the eighteen hundreds."

"Sounds interesting, Conrad. When did you want to go?"

"Saturday sound okay?"

"That sounds fine. And, Conrad, I'm looking forward to seeing you."

"Yes, me too," and he thought, Come into my web, my little blonde fly.

Conrad felt relieved when Saturday arrived. He had spent two days working at the Hill Development Corporation. He had felt much like a fish in a bowl, totally unobstructed from everyone's view. "How are you, Conrad? Nice to see you back, Conrad." It was all he had heard all day long. And then there were those who hadn't said anything but stared, speculating why he had been absent from work, the ones who could breed juicy rumors and gossip. These people, by Conrad's definition, could best be categorized as repulsive scumbags, and he had no tolerance for any of them.

Conrad was at Erica's house at noon. "We have the remainder of the day to let the spirit move us," he said to her.

"Free as a bird," and Erica raised her arms to depict the wings of a bird and mimicked flying.

It made Conrad laugh. "That's good, Erica. I like your style."

"I hope so. I expect to see more of you," she said confidently.

Her words were well received, and he smiled at her." Ready to go?" and he opened the door to the Trans-Am for her to get in.

"What made you think of this place, Conrad?" she was curious.

"I thought it would be a great place to make love," and though he said it teasingly, nothing could please him more. He found her to be such a turn on that it was becoming increasingly difficult not to entertain the thought of going to bed with her.

"It would, would it? And how would you manage making love to me? You're not a voyeur, are you?"

"That's three straight questions, Erica, and I plea for the free spirits help."

She laughed and said, "Let's see if it helps you." Then she asked, "What do you know about this place besides being a prospective haven for making love?"

Construction of the mansion and surrounding buildings was completed in 1868 at a cost of nearly two million dollars. How's that grab you, Erica?"

"It's mind boggling. Two million dollars back then. I'd like to have one million dollars today," and she was amazed by the information.

"I have more incredible facts. The mansion is four stories in height and contains more than sixty rooms and fourteen bathrooms. It even has a central heating plant and a unique water supply system with pipes a half mile long to bring water into the mansion from a private reservoir."

"All that in 1868?" she said surprised. "People were pretty innovative back then. Who were the lucky people to inhabit the place?"

"I guess I forgot to mention it. It was built by Le Grand Lockwood who resided in Norwalk, and who was a financier in New York City, and it was designed by Detlef Lienau, a distinguished Paris trained architect of the Victorian era."

"That's interesting, Conrad. You are a wealth of information. If I were a teacher, I'd certainly give you an A+ for the report."

"You know what blows my mind, Erica? The poor bastard didn't even get to live there for ten years when he died, and Charles Mathews purchased it in 1876. Like I said before, life is an unfair predator. You never know when its fatal talons will grab you by the neck."

"I guess you have a point, and that's all the more reason to live your life to the fullest. I'm really aroused to see this place."

"Me too," he said.

"Thanks for the history lesson," she again thanked him. "Did you know I'm a history buff?"

"No kidding, Erica. I love the subject myself."

"I'm beginning to think you and I are very compatible. What do you think about that?" she asked groping for his feelings.

"It could cause two people to fall in love," and he groped himself.

"That could be dangerous," and she looked at him and smiled.

When they arrived at the mansion, Erica thought it was elegant and beautiful, living testimony to an era gone by.

"And they wanted to take this place down for a stupid, modern day shopping mall," said Conrad. "No respect for history or architectural beauty and excellence."

"It sucks," said Erica in total concert with Conrad.

"That's one of the things I dislike about my work, Erica. The more land that my father develops, the more our woodlands and fields are destroyed reducing the purification of our air supply. It also abates the livable habitat and the food supply of our wildlife. Everything is damn money," and she could see it genuinely disturbed him. "I'm not against progress, but I advocate the concept of open space. In other words, leave a certain amount of land undeveloped for the environment. I don't understand why local government doesn't insist on such a policy."

"We need more people like us," and Erica squeezed his arm in support.

Conrad looked at her and smiled appreciatively. "We better start making babies then."

"A whole lot," said Erica, and she raised her eyebrows waiting for Conrad's reaction.

"I hope they are all blonde and beautiful like their mother."

"Really now, and what about some handsome sons?" she asked.

"We'll manage a few of them too."

"Let's get inside this beautiful structure before we become exhausted from having all these verbal babies," said Erica.

It made Conrad laugh. "Verbal babies," he repeated. "I like your style Erica." Her ability to engage in repartee reminded him of Abigail. She had been so adroit at it, and it was one of the qualities he had liked about her.

Once inside the mansion, they savored every aspect of the interior. The Victorian influence manifested itself in the detail of the fireplaces, elegant staircase, the ceilings, and the wall moldings.

"Just awesome," were Erica's words.

When the tour was over, Erica wouldn't have minded going through it again.

"How would you like to live in a similar place but on a much smaller scale, say twenty rooms and five bathrooms?" asked Conrad.

Of course Erica thought he was kidding. "I'd jump at it. Right out of my shoes. Of course, I'd want a large, beautiful bedroom so I could have loads of real babies," and she fluttered her eyelashes.

"I'll keep that in mind," and he took hold of her hand. "Come on sweetheart, let's go and get something to eat."

"I have a request. Can we get some take out and find a spot in the country and eat out in the fresh air?"

"Would you like that?"

"I'd love it," she said with feeling.

"Then your wish is my command."

"We really don't need anything fancy. Kentucky chicken would be fine," she suggested.

"You got it, Erica. I like an inexpensive date," he teased.

"But I warn you, I like large diamonds," and she held her left hand out extending her fingers making him laugh.

"That's a hand worthy of at least two carats."

"I accept. Do you want to take the hand with you so you can be certain of a perfect fit?"

She was good, so quick and witty.

"Only if you come with it," he replied.

"You could get stuck with me."

"I can handle it."

"Last guy couldn't," she said quickly.

"He obviously was a damn fool," and much to his surprise he said it with feeling.

"I couldn't agree more," she said, and they both had a good laugh. And they had many more laughs during the remainder of the day.

He had tried to convince her to make love in the woods, but she had turned him down. "If we do it now," she had told him, "you will know everything about me physically. This way you will have something to look forward to."

When he tried to speak she had placed her index finger across his lips to hush him from speaking. A moment later she had kissed him gently, looking into his eyes smiling.

When Conrad was back in the condo, he made a drink and sat in his favorite armchair by the fireplace. As was his custom, he laid back and reviewed the events of the day. It had been a good day. Erica had conversed freely, and she had given every plausible indication that she liked him and enjoyed his company. Of course, it was his personal evaluation, but he believed he was objective and honest with it. The resulting conclusion being that he was making excellent progress with Erica.

But one thing puzzled him. For some strange reason he enjoyed himself when he was with her as much as any man pursuing a girl he really cared for. It wasn't that way with Penny. How could that be? Conrad thought when he really wanted to hurt Erica emotionally the way he had been hurt by Abigail.

"This feeling for Erica will pass," he said aloud. She was a personable girl who was fun to be with. And of course, she was very beautiful. That's all it was, and he tried to convince himself the feeling would pass.

$\mathcal{A}$ Flower's by Dawn delivery truck pulled up in front of The Corrugated Box Company. A delivery boy—with an arrangement of two-dozen yellow roses—made his way to the lobby receptionist.

"Are those beautiful roses for me?" the receptionist asked jokingly.

"They are if you're name is Penny Hennessey," the delivery boy replied.

"Penny," the receptionist blurted unable to conceal her surprise.

"Yes, that's what it says on the envelope," he said feeling a need to reaffirm what he had said before.

"Thank you, I'll see that she gets them," her surprise now having turned into curiosity and envy.

A moment later the receptionist had Penny on the phone. "There is something in the lobby for you."

"There is? What is it?"

"I can't say. You have to see it for yourself," and she was decent enough not to expunge the element of surprise that awaited Penny.

"Okay, I'll be there in a bit. Thank you, Lisa," and she wasn't the least bit curious. Probably some computer supplies, she thought.

Later, when Penny went out to the lobby and discovered the roses were for her, she was so overwhelmed she had to sit down. When she opened the small envelope and read the enclosed card that said Have a Great Day, Love Conrad, her eyes began to tear. "I can't believe he sent me such a grand display of roses," she kept repeating, "And here at work." A moment later after she calmed down, she became embarrassed, her shy demeanor and modesty taking control.

"Who is he?" Lisa asked. When Penny hesitated she said, "Come on, Penny, what's his name? You have been holding out on us."

Her embarrassment quickly turned into pride. She suddenly was important to her peers. "Conrad," she finally informed Lisa. "And yes, he is very kind and generous," she said proudly.

"Does he have any brothers?" asked Lisa.

"No, he's an only child. I guess I lucked out."

"From the look of those roses, I'd say you did. I'm actually jealous. My boyfriend gives me one rose at a time. I'll certainly have to tell him about yours when I see him."

Penny giggled like a little girl. "I guess I better get back to my desk," and she picked up the roses that practically obscured her view. When she arrived at her desk, a chain of reaction started among her associates.

"Where did you get those gorgeous roses?" Betty was the first to ask.

"From my boyfriend Conrad," she said shyly, her cheeks flushed.

"Your boyfriend," Peggy Sham said with alarm. "You have a boyfriend?" she couldn't help repeating.

"Yes, I do," Penny said softly. She hadn't had the opportunity to say boyfriend in a long time. And it felt good to say it. After all, Conrad did send roses and his love. It was plausible to now refer to him as her boyfriend.

"But you were so clandestine. We would never have guessed," Betty said with a tone that bordered on indignation.

"Tell us about him," said Cindy. Of all her peers, Cindy was the only close friend Penny had.

"There isn't much to tell. He's good looking, generous and kind," and she really didn't want to offer any more information as proud as she felt.

"Not much to tell. He sounds like a hell of a guy, Penny. I can't believe you held out on me," said Cindy.

"I didn't mean to," she said being apologetic. "I wasn't sure in what direction our relationship was going. I'm sure you can understand that."

"You're forgiven. No need to apologize."

"There is one thing you forgot to tell us Penny. How is he in bed?" asked Peggy causing a stir among the small group of associates.

The question embarrassed Penny. "Please don't ask me that. It's personal and embarrasses me," and she was visibly uncomfortable.

"Back off, Peggy," said Cindy feeling a need to defend her friend. "Use your imagination on that one."

"I have to get back to work," said Penny, and when she was seated she admired the roses on the corner of her desk.

Later, when some of the girls who worked in Penny's department went to lunch, Penny was the center of their conversation.

"Who would find her attractive enough to want to send her two dozen yellow roses?"

"He's probably some kind of nerd," Chris said causing the group of four to laugh.

Peggy, who was extremely opinionated and ruthless when it came to gossip said, "Who the hell would want to make love to that scrawny, flat breasted female with reptile complexion? I'll bet when he kisses her, her pimply chin probably removes his whiskers, and the comment caused the girls to break into guffaw.

"You're cruel, Peggy, so cruel. I'd hate to be your enemy," Chris commented.

"Then watch your ass, girl."

"We really should be happy for Penny," said Dottie showing a little compassion.

"Feel the way you want. I don't think the sordid, haired little mole will be able to keep the guy, whoever the hell he is. I still can't see what he sees in her," and Peggy shrugged. And so the conversation went, with everyone dubious to the seriousness and longevity of Penny's relationship and Conrad's intentions. And ironically, as cruel and vicious as their gossip was, they were right with Penny becoming more and more entwined in Conrad's web of deception.

That evening, Penny received a phone call from Conrad.

"Did you get them?" he asked.

"Are you referring to the twenty four, golden roses that were delivered to me today?" and there was a certain thrill to her voice that couldn't be denied.

"That's correct, my little, silver Penny."

"I love them, and I love you for sending them. I felt very proud in front of everyone. I think it was the proudest moment of my life."

"I'm happy they pleased you, Penny. You deserve to be happy."

"I loved your card," and she hesitated a moment. "I guess you know what I mean," and she hoped she had interpreted the card properly.

"Yes, I meant what it said. I'm very fond of you. I hope you feel the same way."

"Oh, I do," but she was terrified to say she loved him. She had never had the opportunity to say it before. Penny knew the connotation of love meant serious commitment, at least to her. She was ready to respond to the definition, but not totally convinced Conrad was. She was a realist who still lacked confidence in her physical appearance and how others perceived her. And entrenched in her mind the question remained, why did Conrad single her out of all the available girls?

"I'm delighted we understand each other. By the way, when is your birthday?" he asked.

"It's funny you should ask. It's this coming Saturday."

"No, kidding," he said with genuine surprise. "We definitely have to celebrate."

"Okay," she said softly, but she was ecstatic inside.

"I know just the perfect gift."

"You don't have to buy me a gift, Conrad. You already gave me enough. The flowers alone are a gift."

"Nonsense, my silver Penny deserves a lot more. Now that that's settled, I'll pick you up at seven Saturday."

"Okay, Conrad. Thank you again," and she hung up resting her hand on the receiver with an outward sign of affection.

Conrad's phone call reinforced Penny's decision to call her sister Mindy. She had been contemplating calling her before, but she hadn't been convinced she and Conrad had a genuine relationship. Now she was. The events of the day and the phone conversation that just transpired no longer made the relationship precarious. Yes, she would call her.

Mindy was on the phone. "I met the most wonderful guy," Penny informed her excitedly.

"You have," and her sister couldn't conceal her surprise. "When did this happen?"

"About three weeks ago. You'll never believe how we met." Before Mindy could say anything Penny said, "I backed into his car. Weird, isn't it?"

"I guess so. I'd say that's most unusual."

Penny laughed. "His name is Conrad Hill. He's very good looking, Mindy, quite handsome actually, and very kind and extremely generous. He took me to the casino at Foxwood," Penny rattled on. "I never had such a good time. He even said he would take Mom and Dad. Would you believe that?"

"He sounds like someone out of a romantic novel, Penny."

"God sent him to me, Mindy. I've been waiting all my life for someone like him." She was so excited and emotional she had to pause and take a deep breath.

Mindy was suddenly quiet. "Are you there, Mindy?" Penny asked.

"I'm here, Penny."

It was a lot of information for Mindy to digest. And it was totally unexpected, totally. Actually, it sounded too good. Like a plot from one of the many romantic novels her sister had read. All she wanted was for her sister to fall in love, get married to a decent man, and have children. What every girl wanted, including herself. But this new and sudden relationship with Conrad seemed to materialize all too fast and overly zealous, and it aroused her suspicion.

"I'd like to meet this Conrad, Penny."

"Oh, yes, Mindy. I want you to."

"Maybe we can have lunch together."

"That sounds fine, Mindy, and I'm looking forward to it. I'm dying to have you meet him. I know you'll just love him," and her voice was full of certainty.

Mindy thought about it further. "Why don't you call him and see if he can join us the day after tomorrow at the Garden Lunch Stop. That should be enough notification."

"All right, I'll do that. He works at his father's business. I'm sure he can leave any time he wants," she said sounding presumptuous.

"Good. Call me tomorrow, Penny."

"I will. Thanks, Mindy."

When Penny called Conrad his enthusiasm and eagerness to meet them for lunch only enhanced her excitement. Her guardian sister, as she sometimes referred to her, was going to meet her boyfriend, a moment she had wished for with consistency and intensity over the years. To embellish the luncheon date, Conrad was going to pick her up at work where her fellow associates would get to see him in the flesh. The mere thought of it had placed her on cloud nine.

The day of the luncheon, Conrad pulled up to the curb in front of the lobby doors of Penny's work place with his father's new, red Corvette. He had one objective in mind, to peak Penny's emotions and pride. The higher she rides the crest of happiness, the harder she will fall.

Once in the lobby, Conrad said to the receptionist, "Would you please buzz Penny Hennessey and let her know Conrad Hill is here."

"Of course, Mr. Hill," and she gave him a flirtatious smile after being taken by his handsome appearance.

"She'll be right over. The roses you sent Penny were really beautiful," the receptionist said trying to engage in small talk.

"I told the florist the order was very special and that I would see he was rewarded for his extra attention," and he smiled.

"That's very moving to really care like that. Penny's a lucky girl."

He stared at her for a moment. "Thank you. She's pretty special herself."

A moment later, Penny entered the lobby. She was beaming, even though she tried to subdue her pride and happiness.

Conrad greeted her with a kiss on the lips and said, "Hi, Penny."

The receptionist's eyes were locked on them as if her eyes were frozen in place. She had gossiped along with the other non-believing girls, and what she was witnessing appeared to be genuine. And he definitely was no nerd. On the contrary, he was a perfect, physical specimen of a man. She was truly overwhelmed and envious.

Before Penny and Conrad left, a couple of Penny's work associates had conveniently entered the lobby. "Have a nice lunch," they commented, blatantly looking Conrad over like a scanner at a check out counter.

It made Penny chuckle as she left the lobby. And when she and Conrad drove away, she could see a small congregation of girls looking out the windows and doors observing them in the flaming, red Corvette.

Mindy was already at the Garden Lunch Stop when Conrad and Penny arrived. Penny took hold of Conrad's arm as they approached Mindy. She giggled as she said, "Mindy this is Conrad. Conrad, I'd like you to meet my sister Mindy."

Mindy offered her hand and said, "Hi, Conrad. Penny has told me many good things about you."

"I appreciate that. It's a pleasure meeting you, Mindy."

He is handsome, and physically endowed, thought Mindy. But her female intuition raised a flag of suspicion, and her immediate feelings toward him were of reservation and a lack of fondness. She felt guilty feeling that way since she had just met him, especially since her sister was raving about the guy. But she couldn't help the way she felt.

Once they were seated, Penny said, "They have great hot wings here. Great burgers too," trying to initiate conversation. "I don't eat out very often. I usually brown bag it."

"Nothing wrong about being frugal," Conrad commented.

"What do you do for a living, Conrad?" Mindy asked, seemingly ignoring the small talk between her sister and Conrad.

"He works at his father's Development Corporation as an engineer," said Penny proudly taking the liberty to volunteer the information.

Mindy, with a slight frown, looked at her sister momentarily. "I think Conrad can speak for himself."

"Sorry," Penny quickly apologized.

"No problem," Conrad interjected trying to spare her of any embarrassment.

"How long have you worked for your father?" Mindy continued with the topic of his employment.

"Ever since I graduated college," said Conrad.

"Penny told me how you met. I guess first impressions mean a great deal to you since you started dating her right after the brief encounter."

"I guess you can say that. I'm grateful it happened," and Penny looked at him with a huge, grateful smile on her face.

When they were ready to order, Conrad said, "Lunch is on me ladies, so eat well."

"That's not necessary," Mindy quickly responded. "I'll handle lunch."

"No, No, I insist. The least I can do to extend my appreciation for the pleasure of dining with two, such lovely ladies."

He's smooth and a sweet talker. I don't trust him. Not at all, thought Mindy even though it appeared to be a premature conclusion. "Fine, if that's what you prefer," and Mindy's intuition was dominating her actions, actions Penny wasn't at all comfortable with. Her sister appeared to have a chip on her shoulder as the expression went, and she was extremely curious to find out why. The mood of conversation wasn't anything like what she had anticipated.

Half way through lunch Penny excused herself. "Nature is calling," and she left for the ladies room.

Mindy wasted no time interrogating Conrad. She looked at him straight in the eyes and said, "Why are you dating my sister?" and the question was delivered with coldness.

"Because I choose to," he replied looking her straight in the eyes. Contrary to what you may believe, I'm fond of Penny."

"I'm well aware of my sister's physical attributes, Mr. Hill, and you have a lot going for you. Why choose the girl from the other side of the tracks? It's not that she's an heir to some fortune or a physic who can tell the future for gain. Your relationship to me is like a puzzle with the wrong pieces. It doesn't make sense, and quite frankly it bothers me."

"I like the inner qualities Penny has. She is sincere, sweet and innocent."

"That's the problem. She is innocent, sensitive and fragile. I don't want to see her hurt. Not by you, not by anyone."

"Ah, Mindy the protector," he commented. She told me all about you," and he studied her for a moment. Penny's a big girl now. You don't have to play the role of protector anymore," and she was starting to get on his nerves.

"I'll always be her protector, and she'll always be my little sister." Mindy leaned forward and stared at Conrad. "If you hurt her, I'll cut your balls off with a carving knife," and she said it softly but sternly. Her words gave him a strong feeling she wasn't joking. And he thought, the miserable bitch. Who the hell does she think she is talking to me like that? And what nerve to interrogate me. And it was of some consolation to him to know that Mindy would be hurt along with Penny when the time came.

When Penny returned she said, "Have you two become better acquainted?" Conrad and Mindy looked at each other, and then at Penny.

"Definitely," Mindy was quick to answer. "I think we understand each other a lot better, my dear sister," and Mindy gave Conrad a strong stare.

Conrad felt relieved when lunch was over. He had seen enough of Mindy. Even though he refused to let Mindy intimidate him, he disliked her enough to enjoy the freedom from her exposure.

Once in the Corvette, Penny said, "She doesn't look anything like me, does she?"

"No, she doesn't. I'd never know you were sisters."

"She's the pretty one in the family," Penny said in a melancholy way.

And the bitch, he thought. "But I'll bet she isn't as sweet and sensitive as you. Or warm," and he took hold of her hand. "Looks mean crap if you're not good and decent inside Penny. It's obvious you're sister is a strong, willed person. She comes on pretty heavy.

"Did she say something to offend you?" Penny asked concerned. "I want you two to be friends. I would feel horrible if…"

"Relax, Penny," he interrupted. "Everything is fine between us, really. Beside, you're my girl, not Mindy."

She looked at him and smiled, feeling reassured. "Okay, I believe you, my angel from heaven."

"Good, and keep shinning, my silver Penny," and little did she know that she was destined to become a sordid, copper penny.

CHAPTER 21

It was Penny's twenty-first birthday. Conrad was picking her up at seven in the evening. He had not disclosed any plans about the evening except that they would celebrate her birthday. And he was going to present her with a gift that she had told him wasn't necessary. She definitely wasn't a materialistic, oriented girl. She had succumbed early in life to the fact she wasn't destined to be an upper class citizen. She would wait and see what her date with Conrad brought.

It was late afternoon when Conrad stopped at a jewelry store operated by a gentleman he knew. "Is it ready, Chet? I hope it looks genuine and convincing," Conrad said as he approached the counter.

"Just like the real thing," Chet assured him. "One and three quarter carats of pure, cubic zirconia, and just like the real thing," he repeated.

Conrad opened the box and studied the ring. Then his lips broke into a smile. "Great job, Chet," he praised him. Damn good job. Give me the bill and I'll pay you cash." When the transaction was completed and Conrad was ready to leave he said, "Sure beats paying eight grand for a diamond prop. Thanks again, Chet."

While walking to the car, Conrad said, "She's going to love this. Oh yes, she is," and he couldn't stop smiling.

Later in the day, Penny received a phone call. "They asked for you," her mother said handing her the phone.

"Hello," she said into the receiver expecting to hear Conrad's voice. "Hello," she repeated when there was no response. As she was about to hang up she heard a high- pitched, wailing sound. It made her grimace. "How awful," she muttered. "Is anybody there?" and the phone went to a dial tone.

Conrad, being the punctual person he was, was at Penny's house at seven thirty. "How are you Mr. & Mrs. Hennessey?" as they were both seated in the living room when he entered, and the thought crossed Conrad's mind that they were there intentionally.

"Fine, thank you," they recited in unison. "Nice to see you again, young man," said Mrs. Hennessey. Both her parents were delighted he was taking Penny out again. And on her birthday, something they construed as serious intentions.

Knowing Penny had a date on her actual birthday, her parents had celebrated the evening before along with Mindy and her husband.

"Are you ready to go?" Conrad asked Penny. Then he said, "Doesn't she look lovely in that red dress?"

She was wearing a plain, red dress that hung just below her knees. A small, gold cross with a thin, gold chain hung from her neck. Her shoes were red with low heels. What little makeup she wore was hardly noticeable.

Conrad's comment flattered her with her believing it was sincere. And he couldn't imagine how much her parents relished hearing it and savoring the sight of them together ready to embark on a serious date. Their little Penny was visibly happy, so happy at last. Yes, it was truly wonderful.

Once they were alone, Conrad said, "I thought I'd take you to my condo so we can celebrate your birthday alone. I think you deserve a romantic birthday." And Penny thought, what does he mean by romantic?

"I can send out for Chinese," Conrad continued. "Do you like Chinese?"

"Yes, I do," she said.

"Good, then my silver Penny will have Chinese and a romantic birthday," and he smiled at her.

When they arrived at the condo, Conrad ordered a Pu Pu platter, Szechuan chicken, fried rice, and wonton soup and egg roles. And in the refrigerator he had a small, birthday cake with whip cream topping that read, Happy Birthday My Silver Penny.

Penny loved the condo, and even if she had tried to conceal it, she couldn't. Her love of it was blatantly obvious. "I always wanted a house with a fireplace," she told him. Then she walked out onto the balcony where she could see the large pond and bridge illuminated with green and white lights. A zephyr made the water ripple and reflect the surface light against the trees and shrubs that were adjacent to the water's edge, given the appearance the reflections were dancing to the night breeze.

Penny inhaled deeply and filled her lungs with the fresh evening air.

Conrad walked up behind her and placed his hands on her hips. Then he positioned his head next to hers so his cheek brushed against hers. "You like it here, don't you?"

"I love it, Conrad. I feel like I'm on vacation," and when she turned to face him he kissed her.

"Maybe you will have such a place. The future can be full of surprises."

Penny looked at him thinking about what he had just said. Oh, how she wished it would be true. "I'm happy you brought me here. Thank, you," and she was so appreciative.

When they walked into the living room area, the food had arrived and Conrad paid the deliveryman.

"Everything looks so good," said Penny looking the food over. "I haven't had Chinese in a while."

"Then it should taste extra good. It usually does."

And it did. She ate better than the last time in his presence. Her nervousness had abated commensurately with the increased amount of time she had been spending with him. Her confidence and comfort level had also increased inspired by the positive sign of their growing relationship.

When they were finished with dinner, Conrad raised his hand and gestured for Penny to remain seated. "Dessert is coming up for the birthday girl. There is one request, however," he informed her. "You must wear this blindfold for a few minutes," arousing her curiosity. After he secured the blindfold, he removed the cake from the refrigerator and placed three candles on it and lit them, then placed the cake before her.

"Time to remove the blindfold," he said, and Penny had no idea what was going on.

She was surprised to see the cake, and when she read the words on the cake she was moved and became emotional. "Oh, how sweet of you, Conrad, and I thank you so much," and she rose to kiss him.

"Wait, there is more, but first blow out the candles," which she did. Then he placed a small, wrapped package before her. She had never liked opening presents in front of anyone, even as a child. Twenty-one years later she felt the same way, her shyness still prevailing.

Penny slowly, un-wrapped the package, and from its appearance summarized it contained some kind of jewelry. When she raised the lid of the box her eyes became dazzled and her mouth opened. Surprise and joy suddenly raced through her body, and her mind was telling her it was a diamond, and a large one at that. The excitement was over powering, and she momentarily lost her breath.

"Would you like to be engaged to me?" Conrad asked smiling.

She couldn't believe his words or what was happening. It was so fast, but wonderful. No one ever gave her a ring before, let alone a diamond. And to be engaged, it was a trip to the world of the sublime. He hadn't used the word marry, but surely that's what he meant. Her name would change to Mrs. Hill. No, Mrs. Conrad Arlington Hill, to be exact, she thought.

Conrad studied her as she experienced her various levels of emotion. Then he said, "Would you like to be my wife, Penny?"

"Oh, my God, your wife," the realization of what he said grasping her.

"Yes, yes," she cried even though she realized it was all happening so quickly. "I accept your proposal," and she started to cry. He loved her. Yes, he truly must love her to want to marry her. The more she thought about it, the more ecstatic she became.

"I would like this to be an extra, special night, Penny," and he lifted her and carried her into the bedroom, gently resting her on top of the bed.

Her heart started to race at the thought he wanted to make love to her. She had only experienced a physical encounter once before, and it had been as a teenager. The boy had been drunk, and she herself influenced by the alcohol they had consumed. The sexual experience had been quick and unemotional, with the boy thrusting her and then rolling off of her after satisfying himself before she ever reached orgasm.

Now Conrad wanted to make love to her. What if he was dissatisfied with her physical appearance and endowments, and what if she was unable to arouse him? She wondered if he would be able to tell she was sexually inexperienced. Part of her was fearful she wouldn't be able to satisfy him, and part of her wanted him to love her passionately.

"I'm going to make my silver Penny feel wonderful," he promised her.

She looked into his eyes, and when she tried to speak the words stuck in her throat. A moment later she was able to say, "I haven't had very much experience," and her body was trembling.

"Don't worry about a thing," he tried to comfort her. "I'm not going to hurt you. And don't worry about me. You'll do just fine. I promise."

She found his words comforting, and she tried desperately to relax. "I'm sorry I'm so nervous," she apologized.

"That's okay, Penny," he said. And it's perfectly understandable. Why don't you go into the bathroom and freshen up, and I'll get us some wine. I'll be back in a bit," and he smiled at her.

"Thank you, Conrad." He's so good to me. So understanding and considerate, she thought.

When Conrad returned, Penny was in bed clothed with a bra and panties. He handed her a glass of wine and said, "To love." Then he brought his glass to his lips and drank.

Penny's nerves made her consume most of the wine in her glass before she put it down, hoping the alcohol would quickly calm her down.

In a moment Conrad was in bed with her, and she could feel his hands rubbing her shoulders. Then he removed her bra, gently fondling her small breasts. As he started kissing her neck and shoulders, he could feel her body start to stir, and when he moved his mouth and tongue to her breasts and small nipples, she started to gasp and moan. He could sense she was rapidly becoming sexually aroused as she started moving her hands over his back and shoulders. When he started kissing and licking her navel and lower abdomen, it made her start to pant. Then he placed his hands on her small thighs, rubbing them and slowly moving his hands up until he touched her crouch. Her genitals were moist and hot, and he knew she was on fire and ready for intercourse. Without hesitation he slipped her panties off and slid his erected organ into her making her moan, and as he started thrusting her she moaned repeatedly gasping with pleasure, her tongue moving in her mouth.

He sensed she had never had the intense pleasure of a man being inside her, and it excited him. For the moment, all he wanted to do was please her. He engaged himself to maximize her pleasure, thrusting hard, deep, rhythmically.

When Penny peaked at orgasm she cried, "Oh, my God," and she held Conrad tightly, with her breathing intense. A moment later he ejaculated, and she could feel the warmth of his seaman.

What she felt was unprecedented pleasure, and she loved it. Conrad lay next to her. "Does my silver Penny feel good?" he asked.

"Oh yes, Oh yes," she said, her body still feeling ecstatic.

"Me too," he told her, and she felt relieved. She had wanted so desperately for him to be satisfied with her.

Penny lay on her back with Conrad's arm around her, and she could not help but feel her life had been like an ugly painting on the wall that suddenly had become a masterpiece. A masterpiece she hoped she could view and admire for the rest of her life.

The next morning, Penny called her sister Mindy. "Mindy, you'll never guess what Conrad gave me for my birthday last night?" And Mindy had never heard such excitement in her sister's voice.

"From the sound of your voice, it must be something stupendous. Don't tell me he gave you a new car."

"No, no car. It's more elaborate," and she waited for Mindy to guess again.

"I can't think of anything bigger than a car, Penny," and she gave up guessing. She really had no idea, as the last thing that could possibly penetrate her mind would be a diamond ring since she sincerely believed Conrad had no serious intention of marrying her sister.

"So, you give up guessing?" Penny asked. "In that case, my dear sister, I will tell you. A diamond ring with a huge stone, would you believe that?" and the words reverberated in Mindy's head.

No, she couldn't believe it, and she was rendered speechless.

"Mindy, are you there? Say you're happy for me," and it sounded like she was pleading for Mindy to say the words.

"Ah, yes, I'm her Penny," she finally spoke, still dazed by the news. And Mindy thought, why would he buy Penny a ring with a huge stone? Could it be possible he truly loved her? The ring gave every indication he did. But her logic and female intuition signaled something wasn't right. She wanted very much to let Penny know her true feelings without hurting her. She had always protected her, and she felt obligated to continue with the role, especially now since so much was at stake.

"Penny, I want to be happy for you, but isn't your relationship going too fast, especially the engagement part? I mean, how much do you really know about this guy?" and Mindy hoped she would understand why she would be so concerned.

"I thought you would be extremely excited with the news, Mindy," and there was disappointment in her voice.

"I want to be, Penny, believe me."

"I don't understand what the problem is. He's good looking, kind, considerate, and treats me with respect. He has an excellent income and position in his father's business. What else can a girl ask for, Mindy?" and her lack of understanding Mindy was slowly turning into frustration.

Mindy decided to back off. Penny was obviously in love with him and nothing she said was going to change her mind. "I'm sorry, Penny," and she was again apologizing. "I just want what's best for you. You're happy, so I am too." But she wasn't, and she was certain Penny would find out in time what a guile man she had fallen in love with.

"Thanks, Mindy. I know you're happy for me," she now chose to believe. "Mom and Dad are ecstatic. They like Conrad very much."

"That's great, Penny," and I guess that will eliminate mother in-law jokes."

Penny laughed, and then she became serious. "I just thought of something. I haven't met Conrad's parents. Actually, he rarely talks about them. I'll have to get on his case."

"I think it behooves you," Mindy was quick to say. To her, it was another sign to vindicate what she was thinking all along. The man was a guileful phony.

"I'll let you go, Mindy. I'll talk to you soon."

"Okay, and keep me informed of what's going on in your life."

"I will," and she had no idea how much her sister wanted to know.

The next day when Penny went to work, she kept a low profile even though she felt like flashing her ring and screaming out she was engaged. Instead, she waited patiently to see how long it would take for one of her work associates to notice her diamond. To her delight it didn't take Cindy long to notice the ring on her finger while Penny was working on the keyboard.

"Ah," Cindy shouted. "Do I see a diamond on your finger, Penny? What a gorges rock it is, and I can't believe you can be so calm about it, Penny?" and Cindy took hold of Penny's hand and raised it before her eyes to get a closer look. "Shit, what a ring."

"Penny has a diamond?" one of the other girls asked.

"She sure does," and Cindy stretched the word sure.

Chris and Peggy, the gossip queen, were the first to arrive at Penny's workstation. "What did you do to the guy, Penny to get a diamond that quickly? It must have been real good, hot sex," and Peggy's remark made Penny's cheeks become flushed.

"Of course not," Penny defended herself.

"That's some rock, Penny," said Chris.

"Too good," Peggy commented. "You better have it appraised to make sure it's legitimate."

"I would," Chris supported Peggy.

"I can't do that. That would be an insult to my boyfriend. Besides, he can well afford it."

The thought it was real made Peggy so envious she was turning green on the inside and desperately trying not to show it with her facial expression. "I have to get back to work," she said quickly terminating her participation in the attention Penny was receiving.

"Good luck to you, Penny, and I'm happy for you," said Cindy, and the words made Peggy cringe.

How could that homely, scrawny thing get such a diamond? Peggy thought, and her jealousy made her miserable.

For the remainder of the day Penny received more compliments on her ring. The news had spread like wildfire, particularly because the diamond was huge and she was a plain, quiet and humble girl that led an unspectacular life.

But all the attention made up for the lack of it over the past years, and even though she wasn't an attention seeker, it made her feel good and finally important. Yes, she was now important.

CHAPTER 22

*C*onrad was on the phone with Erica Hollis. "How's it going, Erica?"

"Fine, Conrad, I'm happy you called. I have some news for you."

"Good, I hope. I abhor bad news," and he sincerely hoped it wasn't.

"No, it's not bad. Actually, it pertains to me."

"To you," he said curious. "Now I certainly hope it's good."

"Remember the Miss Fairfield County Pageant I won?"

"Certainly, and I'm real good friends with that beauty."

Erica laughed. "You are, are you? Well, it happened an advertising company executive attended and liked what he saw. Me, and what do you think of that?"

She reminded him so much of Abigail the way she conversed, her witty spirit and quickness of response. Yes, she was so much like Abigail, and he hated to admit he loved it.

"Why, that's great, Erica, but clue me in. What exactly does it mean?"

"They want to screen me for possible advertising, both local and national. I'm excited Conrad."

"That's great, Erica. I'm happy for you," and he was sincere.

"The only part I don't like is that I have to go to California for the testing," she continued. "I could be there for two weeks. It would be great if you could come with me."

Her comment surprised him. "There is nothing I'd love more, Erica, but unfortunately I can't get away from work right now. I'd love a rain check though."

She was disappointed, for she had envisioned while in California taking their relationship forward to the point of establishing intimacy. "Sorry you can't make it, Conrad. You certainly have the rain check though."

"Thanks, Erica. Have a great time, and good luck. Please call me when you get back."

"I will. Bye, Conrad."

Erica's news was definitely unexpected. So unexpected he would have to change his plans which meant he would have to refocus on Penny and alter his schedule and bring her down sooner than he had planned. One more date at the condo on Saturday, then the bad news when they met again. Yes, that's how it had to be.

Saturday afternoon Penny entered her house with a bag in each hand after shopping at the mall. She had stopped at Victoria's Secret and purchased some sexy, flaming red lingerie. She would wear it later for Conrad in anticipation of making love later in the evening at his condo. She had never imagined she would go to such a store to buy lingerie. It was for pretty, sexy girls with beautifully, endowed bodies. But now she had a boyfriend and lover, and things were quite different. She had also purchased a new powder, blue dress that was above the knees. And it was all to please Conrad, her angel from heaven.

An hour before Penny was to leave for the condo she had a phone call. "This is Penny," she said, expecting to hear Conrad's voice. Instead, she heard nothing at first, then heavy breathing followed by a high pitched, wailing sound that made her grimace, like the call she had received before. Seconds later there was a voice. Angel in the sky will make you cry. Beware the arrow in the heart, and the phone went to a dial tone.

She didn't know what to think, except it frightened her. It was keen and grisly, and she rationalized it was some prankster getting high on harassing people. Yes, that's all it was, and she would concentrate on seeing Conrad later.

Penny was at the condo at eight in the evening. She was sure Conrad would notice her pretty new dress that was six inches above her knees.

"Why, Penny, don't you look nice," he complemented her, and her face wore a smile that stretched from side to side.

"Would you like to go out for a while?" he asked, not really caring what they did..

"If you don't mind, I'd prefer to stay in and maybe we can have some wine and sit by the fireplace. I feel kind of snuggly," and she giggled.

"That's fine. I like a snuggly girl," and she couldn't stop smiling, anticipating him holding her and ravishing her body with the touch of his hands, making her feel sexual pleasure. She eagerly wanted to feel like the last time they were together, so wonderful and fulfilled. And wait until he sees my bra and panties. He will be so turned on, she thought.

After a couple of glasses of wine, Penny's sexual appetite had peaked. "Would you think I was naughty if I said I wanted to make love with you now?" and her eyes were glazed.

"No, I was thinking the same thing," and the words made her heart race.

When she removed her dress, he noticed her lingerie. She was so different than the last time she was with him. She no longer was timid and unsure of herself. She was more confident and aggressive, and her underwear made a statement she wanted to be provocative and sexy.

"Wow, Penny. I like your underwear. It's a great turn on," and she was burning with unprecedented desire to feel his passion. And when he was finished kissing and fondling her, and penetrating her relentlessly to make her experience repeated orgasmic moments of ecstasy, every beautiful color of the universe had passed before her eyes. Life was beautiful, and she wished it would never end.

She wanted to spend the night with Conrad, but she knew she would feel uncomfortable facing her parents in the morning. Besides, she didn't want her parents to think anything negative about him. When she was ready to leave she said, "Conrad, I had a couple of weird phone calls. I'd like to tell you about them to see what you think."

"Please do."

"The first one consisted of a high pitched, wailing sound and heavy breathing. The second call, which came before I left, was like the first except there was a voice after the wailing sound.

"Did it say anything?"

"Yes, but I'm not quite sure what it meant. It did frighten me though because it appeared ominous."

"What did the voice say, Penny?" and his voice conveyed concern.

"I believe it said Angel in the sky will make you cry. Beware the arrow in the heart."

"I see. I wouldn't be too concerned about it. Some jerk pretending to be a poet. Probably some, asshole," and he dismissed the subject.

"I better leave now. It's getting late." She gave him a good night kiss and started for the door when she suddenly stopped and turned to face him. "Conrad, would you like to come to my house and have dinner with us one night this week? I'll do the cooking, that is if you're not afraid to try it," and she giggled.

"I sure would; what night, Penny?"

"Is Friday okay?"

"Friday is good. And for the record, I'm not afraid of your cooking. You'll do just fine."

He was so good, and he always said the right thing. She considered herself so fortunate to have him.

She was going to cook dinner for her angel from heaven. She was so excited she ran back to kiss him again. "Thank you, Conrad, for accepting my invitation. My parents are going to be thrilled," and she thanked him again.

"This time I'm leaving," she promised, and he smiled at her before she went out the door. Then his smile turned into a stare, and he muttered, "The poor bastard."

The first thing Penny had done on Monday morning when she returned to work, was tell her supervisor she needed Friday off.

"No problem, Penny, you are a good worker who doesn't take much time off," he had told her, which was surprising considering her health history and frequent contraction of colds.

And when Friday morning arrived, she felt like she hadn't slept since the excitement over Conrad coming for dinner kept her sleepless most of the night. But she had taken the day off from work so she could concentrate on cooking dinner, sleep or no sleep, for her angel from heaven who was going to grace her house with his first, official visit.

Of course she was going to get some expert advice from her mother so she could be sure the meal would turn out decent and assure her future husband she was perfectly capable of cooking for him. She had gone shopping and had picked up a roast, sweet potatoes, dinner rolls and fresh broccoli, and of course, all American apple pie for dessert.

"I must prepare a good meal for my angel," she kept telling herself as she worked in the kitchen. "Cindy will be asking me how everything went, especially dinner," she said to herself, an additional incentive to be sure everything came out as well as planned.

Conrad would be arriving at six in the evening, and she knew he was extremely punctual. Dinner had to be ready, and that included her and her parents being dressed for the occasion. At five thirty Penny said, "I'm going to get dressed, Mom. Please keep your eye on things."

"I will dear. You relax now and get yourself ready. Everything will be fine."

As Conrad's arrival time became closer, Penny started to become nervous and worried. What if he didn't like the meal? What if he didn't like her family after he was in their company for an evening? What if and if? All the thoughts made her take a couple of deep breaths and she told herself she was being silly. He was too kind and considerate to do anything like that. Everything was going to be just fine, she told herself. Yes, just fine.

Penny hurriedly dressed into a pink pantsuit, and when she descended the staircase her eyes were busy scanning the living room area to be sure everything was in order. Her parents were already seated on the couch anticipating Conrad's arrival.

When Penny passed the small dinning area, the clock on the wall read six o'clock, and she expected the doorbell would surely be ringing any moment.

"Sit with us dear," her mother offered.

"He'll be here any moment," Penny said, and her eyes were focused on the front door. When the doorbell didn't ring as expected, she started pacing. As she paced she frequently glanced at the clock with the hands now reading six fifteen. "I don't understand it," she said out loud. "He's never late for anything," and she was becoming concerned.

"Maybe he got tied up in traffic dear," said her mother trying to come up with some kind of explanation sensing her daughter was becoming anxious and concerned.

"Maybe," Penny answered not at all convinced it was traffic delaying him, and she was suddenly very nervous. She looked at the clock again, which read six twenty five. "I don't understand it," she repeated shaking her head, and she went into the kitchen to check on dinner. She hoped the delay wouldn't affect it. She had tried so hard to make everything perfect. At the moment dinner was okay she concluded, but she wasn't sure how much longer it could sit.

"Darn, where is he? He has a cell phone, so why hasn't he called?" Penny said out loud as she returned to the living room.

"It'll be okay, Penny," her father tried to assure her. At the exact moment he finished his sentence the phone rang, making Penny run to the kitchen to pick it up. "Hello, this is Penny."

"Penny, Conrad," and he hesitated.

"Conrad, where are you? It's six twenty five," she said, her voice full of concern. "Is something wrong?" she asked not giving him a chance to answer her first question.

"I'm not coming to dinner, and I don't exactly know how to tell you what I have to say," his voice sullen and heavy with an ominous tone. It was enough to shoot fear into her body.

"What are you talking about?" she asked, her breath quickening. "Dinner is ready. What do you mean you're not coming?" her voice conveying disbelief.

"I can't see you anymore, Penny."

"What!" she cried not waiting for an explanation. "What did you say?" her nerves making her repeat the question.

"I can't see you anymore, Penny," he said again. "I'm sorry, but I'm back with a girl I dated before I met you. We had broken up for a while, but we're reconciled now. I'm really sorry if I hurt you," and he sounded so convincing.

For a moment she couldn't speak, his words cutting into her heart, then reverberating in her head causing it to suddenly throb. Her body suddenly felt numb, her brain telling her he was breaking up with her. Her angel from heaven was leaving her.

"No, Conrad. Please don't do this to me. Please don't do this to me," she pleaded.

"It's over, Penny," he said without emotion. "It's over between us."

She started gasping. "I can't breathe," she said into the phone, and he still felt no compassion though he guessed her asthma was kicking in.

"Maybe you're not sure what you feel for this girl," she tried to reason with him.

"I'm sure, Penny. I'm sure."

"But you gave me a ring. You said you love me. My, God, Conrad, what am I supposed to do?" and she became frantic and started to cry. "My, God, what am I supposed to do," she repeated, and she started wheezing, feeling her throat starting to close.

"Accept it, Penny, and go on. Look, I have to go now. You'll be okay."

"Please, Conrad, don't do this. I beg you don't do this to me. Oh, God, please reconsider," and her legs were becoming weak and numb from under her.

"I have to go now. You take care," and he dismissed her and hung up.

"No, No," she screamed out, her chest filled with agonizing pain and her body slowly sinking until she was sitting on the floor with her back against the wall, the phone receiver resting by her side. She was crying uncontrollably, and she was gasping for air. "God help me. God help me," she cried.

Penny's parents had heard her grisly scream. Her mother had pushed her walker as fast as she could and had arrived at her daughter's side. "Penny, my dear, you need air. Take this inhaler," and she handed it to her. A moment later her mother said, "We heard most of the conversation you had. I'm so sorry, Penny," and her mother's eyes were filled with tears, imagining the grief her beloved daughter was feeling.

Penny slowly rose from the floor sobbing uncontrollably, her facial expression somber. The mere sight of her pained her mother.

"Penny, please come sit with us," her mother pleaded.

"I'm sorry, mother, but I have to be alone now," and she slowly walked up the stairs to her bedroom, and with her hand on her chest closed the door behind her. She immediately fell on the bed face down, and she felt like she was in the vortex of a tornado, spinning her and forcing her down. Down into the abysmal pits of darkness where there was no light or life. It was as black as death, and she felt like she had died. And if she hadn't, she wished she had.

CHAPTER 23

When the morning light came into Penny's bedroom, it was as if she didn't see it. Nothing was different from the horrible night before. Conrad no longer wanted her, and now she felt no one did. The new life he had given her was over. It had been short and truly wonderful, but it had now been placed into a casket and the lid suddenly closed. It would never open again. How could it? Her angel from heaven had suddenly died and was gone, never to appear again. Angels came only once in a lifetime, and hers had already graced her. Its light would no longer shine upon her face, and one that had recently given her a new life with purpose and meaning. A light that had given her love and fulfillment and transformed her plain, homely body into something beautiful that had gained her respect.

After lingering in bed for most of the morning, Penny got up and entered the bathroom off the master bedroom. She had taken over the occupancy of the bedroom ever since her parents had to vacate it due to failing health.

Penny looked into the mirror and stared at her image. Her face was drawn from stress and disillusionment, and her eyes were red and puffy from excessive crying. The many pimples on her face were bright red as if they had been dabbed by a brush that had been dipped into crimson paint. She looked so horrible she looked away from the mirror, no longer able to look at herself.

She returned to the bed and covered her head with the bed sheet and wanted to die. After a while, she started to doze when she heard a knock on the door. Her concerned mother had struggled and endured pain to climb the stairs to see how her daughter was feeling.

"Penny, it's your mom. Please have some breakfast. You need to eat."

"I'm not hungry," and she thought about the meal she had prepared for her angel. They never got to eat it. No, not a bite, and she felt like she would never want to eat again, and it made her cry.

"Penny, please let me in. Talk to me," she begged. Let me help you," her mother pleaded, but her daughter would not answer.

Penny did not leave the bedroom for the remainder of the day. That evening there was a hard knock on the bedroom door.

"Penny, it's me Mindy. Open the door," and her command was stern. A moment later the door opened. The sight of Penny broke Mindy's heart, and she took her emotionally, battered sister into her arms and embraced her. "Don't you worry, my dear sister; Mindy will make things better. I promise." Penny found Mindy's words comforting. She had always protected her and made the bad things better, and she hoped in desperation that Mindy could somehow miraculously make Conrad want her again. The mere thought made a small flame of hope rekindle in her heart.

"I want you to eat something, Penny. I'm not going to let you become sick. You're more important than any, damn guy. Do you understand me?" and she placed both her hands on the sides of her sister's face and looked straight into her eyes. "Do you understand me?" Mindy repeated when Penny didn't respond to her first question.

Penny nodded, finally acknowledging her sister.

"Okay, that's better. Have I ever let you down before?"

"No, Mindy," Penny said softly.

"And I certainly don't intend to now," and Mindy appeared so confident and serious making Penny wonder what she planned on doing in her behalf. "I'm going to call later to be sure you have eaten," said Mindy. "If you haven't, I'm going to come and feed you myself," she threatened, and Penny had no doubt Mindy wasn't kidding.

"I'll try, Mindy," she said half heartedly, the best she could do under the circumstances.

"Good, now give me a hug," and they embraced.

The next morning, Mindy was at Conrad's door. When he opened it he wasn't at all pleased to see her. She took three steps in and said, "You dirty bastard," and without warning slapped him hard across the face. She hit him so hard his skin reddened manifesting the impression of her hand.

"You bitch," he blurted. "If you ever do that again, I'll break your hand," he swore.

"You don't frighten me," she snapped. "I'm not like the other girls you can screw around with, like my little sister," and she was flushed from anger.

"What the hell do you want?" he asked her with bitterness.

"I'm going to have your ass if anything happens to my sister. I didn't like or trust you from the moment I saw you. I knew you were trouble. I told you when we met I'd cut your balls off with a carving knife if you ever hurt my sister. Well you have, except now I'm going to give you a chance to redeem yourself," and she walked up to him inches from his face. "You're going to rectify the situation and make my sister's hurt go away. And I don't care what you have to do to do it."

Conrad stepped back. "Is that so? You don't think I'm going to let you threaten me, do you? Be serious, Mindy," he said and laughed from nerves.

"Oh, I'm serious all right. I don't know what kind of game you're playing with my sister, and I really don't care. She is gentle, sincere, and frail. She's also a sensitive person. You're not going to mess with her mind and hurt her anymore. So you will make it up to her and atone yourself. If you don't, I'll carve your heart out. You played with matches, and now you get burned. It's as simple as that." Again she walked up to him. "I'm not fooling, Conrad," and her words were cold as ice. "I expect you to act on it immediately."

He hated her with a renewed passion, the miserable bitch, and he wanted to hammer her into the ground. He said nothing more to her as he watched her leave.

A moment later he poured himself a drink. Then he cussed at Mindy, "The miserable bitch. Her husband must be a wimp. No, an asshole to be married to that tyrant," and he rattled on.

Mindy had made him angry and frustrated, and he walked out onto the balcony. It always had a pacifying affect, the fresh air and the serene view. But he had a hard time calming down. "Mindy can kiss my ass," he muttered. "No way in hell will I do as she says," he continued conversing with himself. "I'm finished with Penny," and he walked back into the den. He had successfully downed another victim, and he would take a breather and wait for Erica to return.

Two days had passed since Mindy had confronted Conrad. He had been rehashing in his mind the conversation he had had with her. The more he had thought about it the more he had loathed the nervy bitch.

Originally, he had no intention to communicate with Penny after his recent phone call informing her he had to end their relationship. But Mindy's unexpected visit altered his way of thinking and necessitated another phone call. He would defy the nervy bitch's ultimatum for him to undo the wrong and hurt he had inflicted on Penny by calling her to clear the air, so to speak, and let her know that the protector couldn't help her this time. He decided it was time to make the call.

When he called, Mrs. Hennessey answered the phone.

"May I speak with Penny, please," and she recognized his voice but said nothing. Still, she became excited speculating it was an encouraging sign that perhaps he wanted to apologize and make amends.

After a slight delay, Conrad heard Penny's voice say, "Hello." Her nerves made her voice break.

"Penny, Conrad here. You're sister came to see me," and he got right to the point. "She is one relentless bitch," and he enjoyed cutting into her. "She can't help you. I'm sorry, but you and I are through. We have no relationship. Please make her understand. Take care of yourself, Penny. Someone is out there waiting for you. Be patient and don't give up yet," and he hung up. And for some strange reason he didn't get the same, intense feeling of satisfaction hurting her as he did orchestrating Abigail's demise.

Penny had held out hope that he would call and try to reconcile the relationship with her. He had called all right, but she never got to say a word. Now all hope was gone. She started pacing, her heart racing with the realization of what he just said. "But Mindy told me everything was going to be all right. She told me, she told me," and she was becoming more frantic. She was crying and walking in a circle as the room appeared to close in on her. Then she slowly sank until she was sitting on the floor, sobbing and rocking, thinking Mindy had failed and abandoned her. Now, no one could ever help her.

For the next week, Penny, by choice, had remained secluded in her room like a prisoner, and surely it had not been a struggle to make such a choice. She had willfully abandoned her position at work, and her return to her place of employment was no longer an option.

Her nights had become all the more unbearable when her dreams had turned into nightmares. She would dream of Peggy and the other girls of the office gossip group pointing at her and calling her Penny the poor pathetic soul, rejected by her boyfriend. And how could any sensible man ever want her. In some dreams she would see herself looking into the mirror and the mirror suddenly shattering due to her ugliness. And worst of all, some dreams had her in bed with Conrad, and when he looked at her the sight of her would make him vomit. Then she would wake up screaming and wishing she were dead. Such was the horrible direction her life had suddenly taken.

One morning, after days had passed, Penny's mother was behind the bedroom door. "Penny, are you awake? Are you awake, dear?"

she repeated. "Penny, your father and I are going to the store. We won't be long, and she left hoping Penny had heard her.

When the car started down the driveway, Penny went to the window and watched her parents pull out of the driveway. Dressed in her robe, she left the bedroom that had been her cloistered sanctuary and walked down the stairs into the living room. She sat on the couch and looked around the room as if she was photographing it with her eyes. Then she raised her hand and stared at the ring on her finger. Yes, she was still wearing it, clinging to a past existence. As she had done before she thought, how could I ever return to work when I no longer have a boyfriend? They will all laugh at me and talk behind my back. Every one will look down on me. Poor, plain Penny has been made a fool of. Mindy and mom and dad will think so too, and she hated herself. She felt ugly, and no one would ever want her. She wouldn't be able to face anyone again, and the thought was unbearable. She couldn't and wouldn't. Love had come to her so suddenly and unexpectedly. Now death must do the same.

Penny rose from the couch and walked by the kitchen until she came to the garage door. Once she entered the garage, she walked over to her car and opened the door. She positioned herself behind the steering wheel and inserted the key into the ignition. She lowered the windows and then laid her head back against the headrest. With tear filled eyes she uttered softly the words, "God, forgive me." Then she started the engine and closed her eyes and mourned her own death.

CHAPTER 24

Mindy was devastated when she heard of Penny's death. When she was informed that Penny had committed suicide, she became livid and held Conrad directly responsible. And she vowed to get even for the loss of her dear sister.

Her first priority was to arrange for her sister's burial since her parents were handicapped. But as soon as Penny was properly laid to rest and her family and friends had all departed, she would deal with Conrad.

The first thing Mindy did was take Penny's ring to a local jeweler to have it appraised. When the jeweler informed her it wasn't a real diamond but a cubic zirconia, it vindicated what she had suspected all along. Conrad had deliberately set Penny up for a hard, cruel fall, but she didn't understand his motive, and she had to find out. One thing was certain. Conrad was guilty and responsible for her sister's death as sure as if he had shot her with a gun.

Two days later after Penny had been laid to rest, Mindy was parked in Conrad's parking lot waiting for his arrival from work. She had been parked for a while waiting patiently like a cougar waiting for prey. As soon as she saw him pull in, she was out of her car and in an instant was standing next to his.

"What the hell are you doing here?" he greeted her totally surprised.

"I just buried my sister, you no good son-of-a-bitch. You should be hung for murder."

"What?" her words catching him by surprise.

"You heard me. Penny committed suicide. Happy now?" and he looked at her, his mouth hung open.

"What, what did you say?"

"Do you want to know how? I'll tell you how," she said not giving him a chance to answer. "She died in her car in the garage of exhaust fumes, a pretty pathetic way to go. And it's all attributable to you, you miserable low life rat."

"Why, Conrad? Why did you single her out?" and her eyes started tearing.

For a moment he couldn't speak. "I… I can't believe it," and all he could do was stare at her.

"I came here with a predetermined motion to carve your heart out," and she pulled a knife from her bag to display it. "But that would be too easy. Instead, I'm going to haunt you every day of your life. I'm going to make you miserable and constantly remind you of what you did to my sister," and her voice was filled with animosity. "When I'm through with you, your going to wish you never knew Penny, and you're going to hate yourself," she threatened him.

"I… I didn't mean for that to happen. I had no idea. I…"

"Shut up!" Mindy screamed. "I don't want to hear any more of your bull shit. You know what would please me, Conrad? If you hung yourself, you lowly bastard," and she walked away.

He felt relieved when she left. He didn't appreciate being verbally assaulted. And for the first time he felt disturbed with the over all outcome of his plot that victimized Penny as an instrument to achieve gratifying revenge against women as a result of sustaining irreparable hurt from Abigail. He hadn't expected her to take her life. No, it wasn't his intention, and he sought solace.

There wasn't anything he could do now, and he tried desperately to clear his head of Mindy's cutting words that were ringing in his brain. It made him hope that her hatred of him would quickly start to erode with time like unprotected soil being removed from the side of a slope by heavy rain.

Later, when he was in the condo, the phone rang. It was Mindy who said, "I want you to meet me at the Holy Family Church two miles from Penny's house at six this evening. And I want you to ask God to forgive my sister for taking her life, and confess to God you were responsible for her actions. I demand that you do this at the altar before the cross," and her voice was unwavering.

He dreaded confronting her. She was making him feel diminutive and causing his conscious to become heavy with guilt. He fathomed she was engaging in psychological warfare to scar him mentally and emotionally, to make him a slave to her commanding desires, and to her punitive actions. Her words I want, I want were starting to penetrate his resistive armor, and it made him weary.

"Let me be, Mindy. Give it a rest. There is nothing I can do to bring Penny back. She's in God's hands, not mine. So leave me alone," and he was pleading.

"Go to hell, you bastard. I told you you were going to wish you never met my sister. It's a small price to pay in contrast to what you did to her. And not for a second don't you think changing your phone number will stop me from haunting you. I'll find you no matter what you do, you bastard."

"Please leave me, alone," and he terminated the conversation by hanging up abruptly. He had had enough, and he didn't have the patience to talk to her anymore. He hated her and he wished he could close his eyes and never see or hear from her again.

At eight o'clock that evening, Conrad retired for the day, totally ignoring Mindy's demand to go to the church. As soon as he had gotten into bed the phone rang. He reluctantly picked it up and said, "Hello," expecting to hear Mindy's voice.

"Is Karen there?" a voice asked.

Conrad felt relieved. It was a wrong number. "You have the wrong number, and as he was about to hang up the voice said, "How about Penny Hennessey?" and it jolted him. Immediately he slammed the receiver down. "That bitch," he grumbled. She was going to be relentless, he concluded. And she obviously planned on utilizing a variety of tactics to wear him down.

He decided he wouldn't answer the phone. The answering machine could do it and screen the caller. Now, all he wanted was a good night's sleep. The day had been extremely stressful, to damn stressful to be exact. He would shut down his mind to everything and not think, and the world could kiss his ass good night. "All I want to do is sleep," he mumbled, and he closed his eyes.

Conrad was dreaming. He was standing in front of a small house badly in need of paint. It looked so familiar. "But why am I here?" he was asking himself. He wanted to turn and leave, but his legs wouldn't let him. Then he heard a familiar voice speaking softly to him. "Come inside, Conrad, my angel from heaven. Come into the garage and join me. Please sit in the car with me."

He didn't want to go, and he was fearful. "The living people don't belong there, and please don't ask me."

"Come to me, my angel," the voice insisted, and he suddenly could feel himself floating, unable to control his body. He floated toward the garage door that turned into a cloud of mist before his eyes. When the mist dissipated he was in the garage standing in front of an old, Plymouth automobile. A girl was sitting behind the wheel. He knew her. Of course he did. He had taken her out. It was Penny Hennessey, the girl they said he had murdered.

He was staring at her face. It was chalk white, and her eyes were melancholy and gray with dark circles. Her lips were dark like the color purple, and the sight of her was frightening him.

"Come in the car with me," and she was gesturing with her hand for him to sit next to her.

"No, no, I can't. I must leave," and his breathing was intensifying while he was dreaming. He was starting to float again, and in an instant he was sitting next to her.

"That's better, my angel. Sit close to me. You belong here with me. When I start the engine you will be with me forever," and she was smiling at him while his body was quivering.

"No, no, Penny, please don't start the car," he begged her. And when he turned to face her, the pupils of her eyes were gone striking fear in his body. She appeared illuminated now, and when she started the engine he bolted out of his dream, sitting up and screaming as if he had been triggered and thrust by some giant spring.

"My, God, it was only a dream, but so real," he said, and the realization made him grateful that's all it was. Perspiration was seeping out of his pores, creating little beads of water all over his body. The nightmare had been so intense that the sheets were wet and quickly had become cold to the touch.

Conrad got out of bed and went into the kitchen and poured himself a glass of wine. "That bitch, Mindy," he cursed. "It's all her fault I had the freaking dream. She won't leave me alone. Christ, I think she's going to destroy me," and he was genuinely worried. He started pacing with the wine glass in his hand, and then paused momentarily to drink some. He filled the glass again with wine, and then walked into the den and sat in the armchair next to the fireplace and looked at the clock on the wall. Its hands were positioned at twelve midnight. "Christ, it's only midnight," he moaned hoping it had been later.

The nightmare had been so real he was for the moment terrified to go back to bed for fear he would dream again. "I can't look at that face again. I just can't. It's so ghastly," he was telling himself.

Conrad rose from the chair and started pacing. "Screw it, I don't need to sleep. I have to stay awake. That's what I need to do," and he turned the television on. It didn't matter what the program was He would watch anything, anything that would keep him awake.

In the morning when Conrad got the first glimpse of the rising sun that would soon eradicate the darkness of night, he was so happy he watched it until it rose above the horizon. He would go to work and forget about Mindy and his nightmare. He was destined to have a good day, for the law of averages was in his favor. "I'm overdue," he tried to convince himself.

When Conrad arrived at work, he was immediately called into his father's office.

"We need the drainage at the Bakersfield Mall to be finalized within the next few days Conrad," his father informed him. "We are ready to proceed with the preliminary grading.

"Sure, father. I'll jump on it right away," and he didn't need the additional stress in his life at the present time. And when he recalled the sabotaged, preliminary calculations he had made in retaliation against his father's threat to cut off his trust income, it only served to compound his stress.

When Conrad left his father's office, Lisa the secretary heard him cursing again. "Shit, who needs this freaking job?"

Conrad had just entered his office when he was buzzed on the intercom. "You have a call on line three, Mr. Hill."

"Hello," he answered strongly.

"You didn't show at the church last night, you scumbag. Don't do it again. Children who play with fire get burned."

"Is that a threat?" he asked forcefully.

"Call it what you want. Tonight at six and don't be late. This is your last invitation," and the phone went dead.

"Bastards," he blurted.

It was a man's voice clearly indicating someone else was involved with Mindy. Probably some sort of bodyguard or co-conspirator he reasoned. "The dirty bastards," he moaned. When was it going to end? His nervous system was on edge. He was starting to realize there was no sanctuary from Mindy, and it was an ugly thought.

At lunchtime Conrad decided to have a quick lunch in the company lunchroom. Several vending machines were lined up against the wall to accommodate the employees. The machines offered a small variety of sandwiches. For those employees who chose to brown bag their lunch, the machines also offered cold soft drinks, hot coffee, and snacks.

As soon as he sat down Charlene Lavoie approached him.

"Mind if I join you?"

"Not at all, he said."

"I haven't seen much of you lately, Conrad."

"I know."

"I miss your company," and she smiled at him. Then she studied him. "You look stressed and spacey. Want to talk?"

They always had in the past. He liked her and enjoyed the sight of her over, endowed breasts. She still possessed her eternal crush on him. They were good friends, and they usually conversed freely.

"Ah, yeah, I've been stressed lately."

"Can I help?" she offered.

He thought about what she said. He had been keeping all the frustrating and stressful experiences to himself, feelings and emotions hankering to be released and vented. "Charlene,"… and he hesitated. "Are you doing anything tonight?"

"Why, no," she was quick to answer.

"How would you like to come over to my condo? I need a friend to listen to me. I can send out for Chinese."

"Sure, I'd love to," and her facial expression lit up. "Just give me the address and the time, and I'll be there."

Conrad pulled out a piece of paper from his wallet and wrote down his address and phone number. He handed her the paper and said, "Seven tonight okay?"

"That sounds great."

"Thanks, Charlene."

"The pleasure is mine," and she was smiling.

Charlene was at Conrad's condo at seven in the evening. "It's beautiful here, Conrad. You should have invited me here a long time ago." She walked out onto the balcony and savored the view. He walked out and joined her. "That's my favorite spot," and he pointed at the bridge and the cluster of graceful Dogwood trees that were concentrated where the bridge met the land. Floodlights lit the bridge and trees with shadows, giving the affect that the trees were cascading.

"I can see why," she commented.

He took her by the hand and led her into the den when she asked, "Looking for a roommate?"

He wasn't sure if she was serious or joking. "Not at the moment, but if I was I would surely give you serious consideration."

"Good, because I would accept," and she was dead serious"

The food arrived, and as they started to eat Conrad said, "I really don't know if I should be talking to you Charlene about what's bothering me. It's my problem," and he paused.

"It's okay, Conrad. You can always talk to me. Whatever you say won't leave this room. You know I'd do anything for you," and she reached out and touched his hand.

"Thanks, Charlene," and her words were comforting. He started to expound. "Abigail broke up our relationship some time ago, and I've had a difficult time adjusting to it. That's the reason I took a leave of absence from work. I don't know if you knew or not."

"No, I didn't. I'm sorry, Conrad," and she looked at him caringly.

"Well, I became so bitter that I got even with her and hurt her badly with the help of a friend. I won't go into all of the details except to say that she experienced the same kind of hurt that I had encountered when she left me."

"That's fine, Conrad. I don't need all of the details," and she was listening attentively.

"Then I found hurting Abigail wasn't enough, and that I needed more satisfaction. So I dated this homely girl named Penny with the intention of deliberately hurting her by dumping her unexpectedly," and he studied Charlene for a moment, wondering if what he told her had altered what she thought of him. "You must think I'm some kind of creep by now?" he asked.

"No, I don't. When you're finished telling me everything, I'll let you know what I think."

"That's fair enough," and he continued. "After dating her for a while, she fell in love with me and that's what I wanted. Then I dumped her hard. Too hard, I guess," and he hesitated looking at Charlene giving the impression that what he had to say was going to be difficult. "Her sister recently informed me that Penny had committed suicide, and she now holds me responsible. I'm having a recurring nightmare about Penny's death."

"Wow," Charlene said, the word flowing out of her mouth. "That's awful. No wonder you're stressed."

"Her sister Mindy keeps calling me demanding I go to church with her and confess before the cross I was responsible for Penny's death. And that I should ask God to forgive Penny for committing suicide," he lamented shaking his head.

"What a horrible burden," she sympathized with him.

"What should I do?" and talking about it didn't make him feel any better.

She found the question difficult as it involved different peoples' emotions. Even though she wasn't personally involved the answer she gave would still reflect to some degree her own emotions. She thought a moment and asked, "Are you a religious person, Conrad?"

"I'm a God fearing person, but not overly religious," he answered her honestly.

"I think it might be a good idea if you spoke with a priest. I get the impression that you have no intention of capitulating to Mindy's request for confession."

"I can't stomach the bitch," and he was unable to control himself. "She rubs me the wrong way. If her attitude had been different at the onset, I might have given in." He was silent for a moment. "But I really didn't make Penny do it, did I Charlene?" looking for her support to relieve his conscience.

"Technically, no you didn't, but indirectly, maybe. You're deliberate scheme was poignant enough to make her want to end her life. She studied him for a moment, knowing he was deeply troubled. "Perhaps you should talk to a priest," she iterated. "I think that's the best course of action for you, Conrad, considering the nightmare and all. You definitely need to get rid of your guilt. I think your dream is telling you that."

He extended his arm and took hold of her hand and squeezed it.

"Thanks, Charlene. Maybe you're right, and that's what I should do. When this thing is over I'm going to take you out, and we'll have a great time."

"I'm going to hold you to that because it sounds good to me. You know I'd love that," and she couldn't conceal her enthusiasm. She wanted to stay and seduce him, but she knew the timing wasn't right. "I'll leave you now, and I'll see you tomorrow at work." She gave him a kiss on the cheek and left.

When Conrad went to bed, he started dreaming. He was in a large room filled with waist, high mist as thick as fog, when suddenly a voice emanated out of the fog. He had heard it before. "Come make love to me, my angel. I wait anxiously for your touch. Please don't disappoint me."

He was suddenly floating, and then hovering over a white casket. "I can't love you. You're dead. Please don't call me anymore," he begged.

"Lift the lid, my angel. Let me feel your magical touch. Open the lid now."

Conrad was stirring restlessly in his bed. Oh, so restlessly as the lid of the casket suddenly was raised. He could see the chalk, white color of her naked body and wizen skin as if she had been dead a long time. Her eyes were gray and sunken into the cavities of her skull. Then he suddenly dropped into the casket, and when he felt the coldness of her body he woke up screaming. It was a grizzly scream, and his body was convulsing from the terror of his dream.

"God help me," he wailed. "God help me." His body was again saturated, just like the last horrible nightmare he had had. Even his hair and scalp were drenched with perspiration. He got out of bed and washed his face with cool water. Then he looked at his face in the mirror and saw the reflection of a frightened man. One thing was certain, the nightmares had to stop or he would surely be destroyed.

CHAPTER 25

When morning arrived, Conrad had not slept a second since he had awakened screaming from another nightmare. He was exhausted, and he decided he wouldn't go to the office. There was always tomorrow.

After eating a light breakfast, he decided to go out on the balcony and search his heart and soul. The time had come for him to evaluate what had transpired in his life ever since Abigail had left him. He recalled the conversation he had had with Charlene. Perhaps Charlene was right, and he should see a priest and ask for forgiveness. Maybe he had been a vindictive bastard that should have let go at the time and gone on with his life in a constructive manner. Again he recalled Charlene's words. She was probably right about forgiveness being necessary for the eradication of the nightmares. They were starting to control his life. There could be no restful sleep, and with out sleep his health and mental stability would surely deteriorate. Yes, he would ask forgiveness for his own actions and Mindy could go to hell. His business was between God and himself, and not Mindy, who would make it a threesome.

In the afternoon, Conrad entered St. Christopher Catholic Church and sat in a pew at the rear of the church. He felt uncomfortable and conspicuous, and he looked around realizing he was alone. He knelt down, and a moment later he heard footsteps behind him.

"I was waiting for you," and he recognized Mindy's voice.

"What?" he said shocked. "What are you doing here? How did you know I'd be here?"

She ignored his questions. "It doesn't matter where you confess, as long as you do it."

"I've done nothing wrong. Leave me alone," he insisted.

"Then why are you here?" she asked, and he did not answer. "You look like hell," she said. "Dreaming of my sister?" and he wondered how she knew. "You'll feel better if you confess. My sister won't rest in peace until you do. She'll haunt you for the rest of your miserable life, and so will I. Is that what you want?"

"No, I don't," he confessed, and his voice broke. She was wearing him down, and he had no doubt she and Penny would continue to haunt him and put him through hell. He didn't want to dream anymore, and he decided he would capitulate to Mindy. He rose from the pew and walked slowly until he stood before the altar. Then he kneeled down before the cross. She was standing behind him when he looked up at the face on the crucifix. Then he suddenly became cognizant of the pain and suffering his God had endured. The horrible pain of the crown made of thorns that penetrated his skull and brain, the agony of nails through the wrists, and then hanging until he could no longer breathe.

Conrad's eyes were watery as he felt the grief as he had never felt before, thinking of what they had done to his God. And they began to tear when he thought about his own misery, so diminutive in comparison, but nonetheless real pain that penetrated his body. His God was guilty of nothing, but he was guilty of willfully manipulating the lives of people so that they would feel pain. Yes, guilty he concluded, and it pained him to admit it.

He made the sign of the cross and then spoke. "My God, please forgive Penny Hennessey for her act of suicide. I was responsible because of the way I treated her. Please," and his voice broke, "let her reign in your kingdom in paradise," and he made the sign of the cross. Then he turned and looked at Mindy, his eyes full of tears.

See, that wasn't so difficult," she said with a sense of relief. She stared at him as if she was pondering more commentary, but reconsidered. A moment later she turned and walked out of the church, and he couldn't believe she was gone.

Conrad was sobbing when a priest approached him. "May I help you, my son?"

He looked at the priest and wiped the tears from his face. He hadn't been to confession in a long time and hadn't talked to a priest just as long. His first emotion was embarrassment, and then he felt shame.

"Is there anything I can do for you, my son?" the priest offered knowing he was troubled and in obvious need of understanding and compassion.

"Father," he started to speak and then hesitated.

"I'm Father Francis, my son. Here, come sit," and with his hand motioned to the front row.

"Thank you, father," Conrad said softly.

"Our conversation is sworn to secrecy," Father Francis assured him not knowing what was troubling him.

"I know," and he sat in a stooped position that reflected his grief.

"What is bothering you, my son?" Conrad's hesitancy to speak made him ask again.

"A girl I loved very much suddenly decided she didn't want me anymore. I have been very angry and vindictive with certain people because of it, and I hurt them emotionally. One girl was so distraught as a result of my deliberate manipulation of her emotions she committed suicide." He paused a moment, breathing deeply in an attempt to relax himself. "I want and need peace of mind father," Conrad continued. "I don't want to live with guilt anymore. But I feel anger when I think about how I was hurt," and he let out a deep sigh.

"You need to ask God's forgiveness, and he will forgive you just as you must forgive those that hurt you. God loves you. He loves all his children. Our Lord will wipe your slate clean and give you a new beginning. Then you must make your heart small enough so there will be no room for hate, and large enough so there will always be room for love. You must also forgive yourself, my son."

Father Francis studied him for a moment, and it appeared Conrad's expression of grief and despair had lightened as if his burden had been eased. "No man is perfect and without sin, and your God knows this," Father Francis continued. "This is why his most important message to all of us is to love each other, and ourselves. If we do this and love our God, we can only live much happier and fulfilled lives, my son."

He wanted to believe everything Father Francis was saying. His words were highly motivational, and he was in desperate need of motivation and inspiration to get his life back. He had strayed from a life of love to one where he had experienced tenure of hatred and revenge. He had become the devils advocate. And for the first time in months he realized how badly his conduct had hurt people, some of whom he had loved and cared about. He had never considered himself to be a bad person, but he had been.

Conrad sat up straight in the pew, his body suddenly feeling energized as if his soul had been starving and it suddenly had been nourished.

"Father, thank you for taking the time to speak to me," Conrad said with humility. "Your words have given me new faith. I think I will now have the courage to try to turn my life around.

"Keep your faith, my son, and God will give you the strength you need."

"Thank you again, Father," and Conrad shook his hand.

When Conrad exited the church, he was grateful and pleased he had made the decision to go to St. Christopher's. He couldn't believe what had transpired there in such a short time, and he felt like his being had been transformed from pain and obsession for revenge, to inner peace and love. It was as if some miraculous dream had become a reality. A dream that put Penny Hennessey to peaceful rest, and a dream that finally eased Mindy's pain and expunged the contempt she had held for him. Yes, he was grateful, and he was anxious to get on with his life.

When Conrad returned to his condo, he noticed the light was blinking on his answering machine. When he pressed the button he heard Erica's voice.

"Conrad, this is Erica. I'm flying out of LA today, and I'll be home late. I'll call you tomorrow. I'd love to see you. I really missed you. I'll tell you all about the trip when I see you. Bye now."

He was thrilled to hear her melodious voice. Erica Hollis, the target of my revenge, he thought. But now she would become the target of his love. Now it was permissible to think about it, and it made him feel good.

The next message played on the answering machine was, "Conrad, this is dad. I need the finalized, engineering drainage report for the Bakersfield Mall tomorrow. It's urgent son. Call me as soon as possible."

"Don't worry, father," he said aloud. "I won't fail you this time," and his dedication was no longer tepid.

CHAPTER 26

"I won't take no for an answer," Barbara Willis was saying." Three days in LA will do you good, Abigail."

"You sure are persistent, Barbara. I guess you are going to badger me until I capitulate and say yes," said Abigail.

"You got that right. Seriously, Abigail, come with us. Roy feels the same way," and she looked at Abigail with innocent, pleading eyes, like a child would at their mother when they wanted something dearly.

"How can I resist those large, pleading eyes," said Abigail smiling. "You win, I'll go."

"That's great, and I'll tell Roy to make the arrangements immediately," Barbara said with delight. "You'll love the company jet. Hey, I have to run. I'll call you, Abigail. I'm truly excited that you're going. Bye, baby."

She owed her life to Barbara. If she hadn't come over to her apartment that morning she would have bled to death. She could talk and think about it now. She had spent six weeks in the mental health facility recovering from the worst experience of her life.

Abigail would always be grateful to Dr. Greta Bron for her dedication in treating her during her recovery from the breakdown. Yes, she could talk about it now, and she thought about Ed often. She had come to terms with the fact she would never see Ed again, even though she still managed to keep a spark of eternal hope inside her that someday something could happen to the contrary. During her sessions with Dr. Bron, Abigail had realized she could never again surrender her heart in the same magnitude she had surrendered it to Ed. He would always own a part of her.

Dr. Bron had instilled in Abigail a new philosophy of life. Address it one day at a time. Eventually, she would experience love again, and her amicable, amorous, extroverted personality made it inevitable.

Abigail had just been released from the mental health facility. She hadn't been to work or out in society for six weeks, and it was the main reason Barbara wanted her to go to LA. Get her back into circulation where she could focus on the present and not dwell in the past.

When Abigail boarded the International Pharmaceutical Corporation jet, she was very impressed with its size and accommodations. It was the first time she had ever been on one. The jet seated eight people, had a workstation, a small bar and a dinning area.

A moment later, Abigail was introduced to Jon Pelletier, the Chief Executive Officer of the west coast division of the pharmaceutical giant. Jon was a man in his late thirties, recently divorced, and a workaholic by every standard of the word. His hair was jet black, and he had chisel like facial features and dark piercing eyes. He was extremely energetic and orderly, and his confidence bordered on arrogance.

"Hi, Abigail, I'm pleased to meet such a lovely woman."

"Pleased to meet, you, and I thank you for letting me join you on this flight."

"You're most welcome. Roy and I go back a few years. We have one mutual interest. We enjoy work, and we're in concert with the phrase of the unknown philosopher who said, "Work is the grand cure for all the miseries and maladies that ever beset mankind."

"Yes, indeed," agreed Roy.

Barbara coughed deliberately. "Hold on here, guys. The reason your philosopher remained anonymous was because he was full of crap," and Barbara looked at Abigail with her eyes conveying the message that Roy being a workaholic was one of the things she hated about their relationship. "Too damn much travel," she would say which made her lonely at times.

Also on board was forty-five year old Gary Peters who was a retired airline pilot now employed by International Pharmaceutical to be on call to fly their aircraft whenever travel was necessary; and the last person on board was Jon's administrative assistant Twi Chen, a young Asian girl with the face and body of a model. She had glistening, black hair that hung the length of her spine. There was no doubt in Roy's mind that Twi was in Jon's bed more often than not. "More power to him," was Roy's sentiments on the matter.

It was not uncommon for Jon to occasionally make exceptions permitting certain individuals to bring a guest or family member on board when they embarked on business trips.

Barbara had met Jon before, but not Twi. "Where are you from, Twi?" Barbara asked.

"I'm from San Francisco. That's were I met Jon," and she looked at him affectionately.

"That's correct," Jon joined in the conversation. "We started talking and I was impressed with her intellectual capacity. Then I hired her. End of story."

"Interesting," commented Barbara.

"What kind of work do you do, Abigail?" Jon asked shifting his attention to Abigail.

"I'm a secretary to the Vice President of marketing for a direct mail company," she informed him.

"I see. We are always looking for good employees. We have a marketing company in New York City. If you like the west coast and you're considering relocation, give me a call," and his comment took her by surprise.

"I'll keep that in mind, Mr. Pelletier," and she wondered if he made the offer to all the pretty girls.

"Jon," he quickly said. "Please call me Jon."

The jet took off a short while later, and to Abigail's delight the flight was extremely pleasant and encountered only a few, mild pockets of turbulence. She wasn't particularly fond of flying, but she had no precluded notions on what to expect on such an aircraft.

Jon had kept them adequately entertained during the course of the flight, expounding on his numerous business trips that brought him to all parts of the world.

Abigail liked him, but not once did she ever fantasize or entertain a thought about dating him. Ed's influence was still heavy in her mind and heart, and she wondered if she would ever feel differently.

Once the company jet landed, the group checked into the Sheraton Hotel on the out skirts of LA. Abigail had a room next to Barbara and Roy, and not trying to be presumptuous, suspected Jon and Twi would be sharing one.

Jon insisted on taking everyone to dinner, and in the essence of time dinned at the Sheraton. Jon pulled out all the stops when it came to ordering appetizers and wine, and he made his dinner companions feel extremely comfortable. Abigail was certain of one thing. Jon's expense account was going to be utilized to the fullest during the trip.

The next morning, Abigail was awakened by the telephone. Upon answering, she heard Barbara's voice. "Wake up, sleepy head. It's ten o'clock, and I'm assuming you're still in bed."

"I am, as a matter of fact."

"Then I'm glad I called. Get your beautiful ass up and moving. We are going on a tour in less than an hour. So get moving, honey."

"Okay, Barbara. I wouldn't want to get court marshaled I'll be ready."

"Good, and good bye," and Barbara was brief.

Abigail stretched and yawned. "I need a minute to wake up," she said to herself, and she took hold of the remote control and turned on the TV. "Let's see if I can get the weather," and she clicked through some channels with no luck. "I'll call the desk," she decided, and before she could pick up the phone it rang.

"Abigail, it's Barbara," she said before Abigail could say hello. "We are going to Beverly Hills to tour the stars homes. I just wanted to let you know. Get ready, and I'll see you in a little while."

"That girl," Abigail laughed. "I must be her only friend, the pain in the ass."

She undressed quickly and went into the shower. She had left the TV on and it was tuned to a local station. When the commercial was finished, the children's show Eddie M and Little Laffy returned.

"What do you say we have a mind reader as a guest on our next show, Little Laffy? I think our viewers and audience would enjoy that," said Eddie M.

"And who's mind are they going to read?" asked Little Laffy.

"We could start with yours," Eddie M answered him.

"That makes a lot of sense. My head is hollow. Did you forget I'm a dummy, dummy?" and the small studio audience of children burst into laughter.

"Okay, you don't have to be insulting about it."

"Then give me a brain, dummy," and Little Laffy gestured with his hand to the children to cheer him on. There was more laughter.

"Okay, okay, little guy. I won't have the mind reader read your mind. I couldn't find a small enough brain for you anyway," and the children laughed at Eddie M's remark.

For one quick moment the laughter spun him back to the past, and for an instant Abigail appeared as a vision before him, smiling and cheering him on.

And ironically, as the children in the studio and the TV audience laughed, no one was aware that Ed McDowell, the man behind the clown who enjoyed making children laugh, harbored a broken heart that was crying on the inside.

When Abigail was dressed and returned to the room, a talk show was in progress that followed Ed's show which had just concluded. She was unaware fate had just dealt her another losing hand. Yes, she had missed the children's show by minutes, and Ed McDowell and Little Laffy were gone once again.

CHAPTER 27

When the Boeing 727 jet touched ground at Kennedy International Airport, Erica Hollis felt relieved. She was an hour from home, and her attachment to the cliché Home Sweet Home had a new vitality. Even though she had been divorced for three years and owned a condo, she spent a great deal of time with her parents and younger sister Debbie. It was not uncommon for Erica to stay at her parent's home for various periods of time, much to the delight of everyone.

During the drive from the airport, Erica formulated tentative plans for her and Conrad. Since she didn't have to work tomorrow, she could call him and invite him to dinner at her parent's home. Besides, it would be a great opportunity for her to make him aware of her cooking skills. And she was anxious for him to meet her parents. What better way was there to a man's heart than a delicious, home cooked, meal. Of course, good sex would help, but she would save that for a more appropriate time.

At nine o'clock the next morning, Erica called Conrad at work. "I'm sorry, but he's not at work today," Charlene informed her.

"Thank you, and have a nice day," and she would try to reach him at his condo. Erica was delighted when she heard him answer the phone. "Conrad, this is Erica."

"Erica, you're back," and she heard the excitement in his voice. "How was California?"

"Great, but I'm happy to be home. How are you doing?"

"Truthfully, I'm bogged down with a high, priority drainage project for the Bakersfield Mall. I have to complete it today. That's why I'm working at home to minimize the interruptions."

"And here I am interrupting you."

"No, you're not," he quickly responded. "You can never be deemed an interruption."

"Flattery will get you every where, Conrad. I confess my original call was to invite you for dinner tonight so you could meet my family and we could see each other, but since the timing is bad we can put the invitation on a back burner," and she concealed her disappointment. She did realize it was a sudden invitation, but her desire to see him over ruled her logic.

"I'm sorry, Erica, but I'd love to come another time," and he meant it.

"I brought you something from California. Nothing big, just a little reminder I was there thinking about you."

"That's so sweet of you."

"Maybe I can stop over around eight tonight for just a short while. I really would like to see you."

"Sure, I'll take a short break. I really don't expect to have the drainage plans completed by then, but please come, Erica."

He was fully cognizant of the fact he could have had the evening free if he hadn't deliberately sabotaged the drainage engineering when he had had words with his father. He regretted it now, and he hoped he would never again be consumed with such vengeance and animosity.

"Great, I'll be there," and he could hear the enthusiasm in her voice.

Erica's eagerness to see Conrad made her arrive at the condo fifteen minutes before the hour of eight.

"Erica, how nice to see you," and he hugged her and gave her a long kiss.

"That's a nice welcome," she said smiling broadly. "Here is the little something I told you about."

Conrad opened the box and removed two T-shirts. One had a picture of Erica across the front, and the other the words I love California.

"I love them, Erica, and I'm honored to wear your picture. Thank you so much," and he was visibly pleased.

"Now, I'll be close to your heart, and there will be no excuses," and she smiled at him.

"You mean there's hope for me?"

She laughed. "I think that depends on you."

"Well, then, maybe I should have a shirt made up so you can wear my picture close to your heart."

"I must admit I was hoping to get the real thing."

He hesitated before answering her, taking her comment to mean she definitely wanted to take their relationship to a serious level, and it definitely was what he wanted too. "I'd say things are looking good in that direction, very good, as a matter of fact."

"I'm thrilled," she said, her eyes sparkling with joy.

"So tell me, Erica, succinctly in the essence of time, what are your chances of becoming a star?"

"I'd say they were very good, if I slept with several of the right people. But if I want to take it at a lower level without sleeping here and there, chances are good," and he assumed she must have felt some disappointment.

"I see," and he was grateful she had that righteous attitude. He wanted to be the one to sleep with her, only him. "I admire your principles, Erica."

"As I mentioned to you before, I would give it all up, if things should work out for me, for a good marriage with Mr. Right. And have beautiful children and a close family life."

"That's a most commendable dream, Erica. I'm sure it's universal and shared by most women."

"When I see you again, I'll tell you about the good things that I experienced in LA. I better go now. I don't want to, but you have a job to finish. She gave him a kiss good night and headed for the door. Before she left she said, "Call me Conrad.""

"I will, Erica. Tomorrow will be a better day for us. Thanks again for the shirts."

She was gone, and he wished she could have stayed. Conrad completed the Bakersfield Mall drainage engineering report at midnight. He was tired and anxious to go to bed, but as tired as he was, he couldn't get Erica out of his mind. He was looking forward to the weekend and relaxing and spending time with her. He couldn't help thinking about the conversation they had had earlier in the evening, which gave every indication the sky was the limit for their flourishing relationship.

Once in bed, he fell asleep quickly, and later in the night he started to dream.

It was misty, and a woman was approaching him from a distance. The mist prevented him from distinguishing who it was and it left him wondering. When she came closer he recognized her, the woman he called lady luck he had met at the casino.

"Are you seeking me?" she asked him, and he felt uncomfortable with her question and didn't know why.

"I don't know," he answered her.

"You want to know what the future holds for you. You want to know about the blonde you hold dearly in your heart," she informed him.

"I suppose," he said still feeling uncomfortable.

"Give me a possession of hers."

"I don't have any."

"I need something she has touched or handled if I'm going to help you. My power will be stronger," and she stared into his eyes.

"There is something," he suddenly realized. "I have a shirt she has touched," and Conrad gave her the shirt with Erica's picture.

"This is good," and the physic held it against her body, concentrating with her eyes closed. Moments later she opened her eyes and studied him. "She loves you. She loves you very much."

"What else do you see?" he asked before she could speak.

"I see," and she hesitated.

"What is it?" and he was impatient.

"I see …, I see you harming her."

"What! How can you? I would never harm her. Perhaps you are seeing another blonde I know. Her name is Abigail. I wanted to harm her. You are seeing her," Conrad insisted.

"No, the girl I see has a letter E in her name."

"You are wrong. What kind of physic are you?" and he was becoming stressed and angry.

"I see what I see," she said with indignation.

He was angry now. "Go away and leave me alone, you fool. I will never harm her, no never," and he stirred restlessly in his sleep until the dream vanished.

CHAPTER 28

In the morning, the first thing he did was recall his dream. "Thank God, it was only a dream," he said shrugging it off.

Conrad quickly decided on an itinerary for the day. He would deliver the engineering report to his father. It was Saturday, but his dad and other personnel were working and expecting the report. He would drop it off and then return to the condo and call Erica. They could go out later in the evening. When she had left the condo last night she had requested that he call her.

It was ten o'clock when Conrad picked up the phone and dialed.

"Hello," a voice answered softly.

"Hello, may I speak to Erica, please?"

There was hesitation before the voice said, "She can't come to the phone." Again there was hesitation. "I guess you don't know. Erica was killed last night in an auto accident."

"What?" he said, unable to comprehend what he had just heard, "What did you say?" he repeated nervously. "Who is this?" and his voice was now frantic.

"Debbie, Erica's sister."

"My, God," he cried. "It can't be true," and he heard Debbie sobbing. "I'm sorry Debbie," and he paused. "I can't talk now. I just can't," and he hung up.

His head started spinning and his heart palpitated making him cough. The word killed was reverberating in his head. "Killed?

Killed? How could it be?" his brain was asking. His sudden shock was turning into grief, and it made him weep. Moments later, when his being had absorbed what Debbie had said his grief had grown into hatred for God. He looked up and shouted, "God damn you. God damn you," he repeated in anger. "What have you done to her?" and he held God responsible. A feeling of helplessness and defeat and emptiness swarmed over him, and he wept bitterly.

He wept for Erica, and the pain made him also weep for all the grief he had recently experienced in his life. And when he couldn't cry anymore, he decided to get wasted. He drank excessively, and then lamented and cursed at God. When evening came he was so drunk he passed out on the floor of the den.

When morning arrived and Conrad awoke, he was sick to his stomach. As a result, he spent the first fifteen minutes of the morning in the bathroom vomiting.

He had experienced many heavy drinking days after the break up with Abigail, but yesterday had been one of the worse days of his life, and his consumption of alcohol had been out of control. It was a day where death had defied him and had taken the girl he cared deeply about.

When the vomiting ceased he took a shower, but he didn't feel much better. He wasn't hungry for food, but he was thirsty. Tomato juice appealed to him, so he poured himself a large glass and drank it.

Conrad's body had no motivation, Erica's death expunging any desire or ambition he may have had. All he could do was meander restlessly back and forth through the condo and the balcony. After a period of such behavior, he sat slumped in the armchair by the fireplace not moving, staring into space reminiscent of a catatonic schizophrenic. For a long spell he was brain dead, unable to think or function, his being in denial and unable to cope with the reality of Erica's death.

Later in the day the phone rang, and the persistence of the ringing penetrated his lifeless state making him again cognizant of the untimely death of Erica and the grief associated with it. He had no choice but to face it, but having to accept it was another issue.

The ringing of the phone activated Conrad's mind, as if fate had decided it was time for him to abandon his brief, quasi state of catatonic schizophrenia.

He couldn't help but wonder about the fickle and volatile aspect of life. Just days ago he had found peace and new faith in religion. Father Francis had assured him God loved him, and he firmly believed everything he had told him. But now Erica was dead, and to make matters worse, her death was senseless. Oh, so damn senseless, and he vowed never to love again.

Conrad strained his mental faculty trying to reason. He had to try to reach some kind of conclusion for the preservation of his sanity. Was God testing his new faith? If so, why make Erica a pawn in his testing game, and in the process take her life? She was totally innocent and yet punished for his behavior. And what was the purpose of the inequality of God's timetable on the human life span? Why did some people live to be ninety and others die as infants, and still others have their lives truncated in their prime? So many questions and no answers, and he mentally had become drained and frustrated.

Conrad got up from the armchair and poured himself a glass of wine, then paced a moment before returning to the chair.

He continued with his effort to try and reason with the latest developments in his life. The image of Christ on the cross appeared before him, and then quickly changed to his own image. Seeing his image like that was so disturbing that he began to perspire. Then he realized the vision was indicative of his carrying a new cross, the burden of which was Erica's death and the consequences he would eventually have to face and handle. The realization made him angry. He could only construe that God was sadistic and cruel and hated him. What else could he think?

Conrad rose from the chair and poured himself another glass of wine. Then he walked out onto the balcony where the cool air brushed against his face. The sun had already set, and the darkness which he hated, added to his despair. His quote and belief that life was a predator and people are prey was vindicated by the latest turn of events in his life, except now he could augment it with more truth. He now considered birth to be a person's crime, and their sentence to be life. And he sincerely believed no one could possibly contest it, no one.

The next day brought more anxiety to an already stressed Conrad. It was inevitable Erica was going to be waked later in the day, and buried on Monday morning. As much as he wanted to pay his respects to her, the mere thought of seeing her lifeless body lying in a casket was overbearing. It was a horrible dilemma he was faced with, and he had no idea how he was going to resolve it. He knew he would feel terribly guilty if he didn't attend the wake, and it made him wonder if he would be plagued with horrible nightmares. He had had his share with Penny, and they were still freshly embedded in his memory.

First, he had to be sure Erica was going to be waked and where. The information would be in her obituary, and when he found it in the newspaper he was so distraught his hands began to tremble. It didn't seem possible to see the name Erica Hollis at the top of an obituary column. She was so alive and vibrant just days ago. Oh, how her death made him hate life.

Erica was being waked later in the day from seven to nine in the evening according to the obituary. Her funeral was scheduled for ten o'clock Monday morning.

Conrad placed the newspaper in the magazine rack next to the armchair and seated himself. He had to make up his mind, and he had to do it now. He definitely wasn't an advocate of procrastination, and his indecisiveness was making him angry with himself.

Erica's death had a poignant affect on Conrad's emotions, and being an individual who felt emotion intensely, it surprised him how much he had cared about her. Right now he was at war with his emotions, desperately trying to control them, just as he had tried when Abigail left him and he had felt her crushing blow.

Conrad rested his head back against the cushion of the chair and placed his lower arm across his forehead and tried to think. He knew the proper thing to do, and that was to attend the wake. It was simple, but he couldn't do it. He couldn't capitulate to the thought of seeing her in the cold grasp of death, the grasp that took his life away too. And if for some reason Erica's casket remained closed, it wouldn't change his feelings. He wasn't going to the wake. He just couldn't.

When Monday came, Conrad was more tired than the day before. He had experienced a restless night, thinking about the funeral every time he awoke. He had reluctantly decided to attend the funeral, that is, go directly to the gravesite and observe the ceremony from a short distance.

He had never met Erica's family, and the thought saddened him because it was something she had wanted. She had wanted to cook for him so he could come over for dinner and meet them. But he had to work late that night. Work late because he had deliberately messed up the engineering project for the Bakersfield Mall to get even with his father, and oh, how he regretted it now. She never would have come over to his condo that night, and the guilt-ridden conclusion of course was that she would be alive today. Clearly, he blamed himself.

Conrad showered, but skipped breakfast because he had a nervous stomach that squelched his appetite. He couldn't understand why he felt so nervous. It wasn't the first funeral he was attending. True, because of his feelings for Erica, he was overly emotionally involved, but something else was bothering him. He couldn't quite put his finger on it, and he decided to loosen up with a drink. He drank it quickly, and then poured another.

Now it was time to sit in the armchair and relax for a moment, and he placed his head on the cushion. After resting briefly, it dawned on him the significance of what he had dreamt the night Erica was killed. The physic he had met in the casino had appeared in his dream. She had told him he was going to harm Erica, and he had argued telling her she was incorrect, and that he would never harm her. But now he realized the physic was right about her prediction.

He did harm her, not deliberately, but in a different capacity. He harmed her with hatred and vengeance, and they were just as deadly as a crashing vehicle. He had to work, so she came to see him, and it was all so unnecessary. If he only had not sought revenge against his father, perhaps Erica would be alive, and the recurring thought had become a fixture in his mind. His conscience was laden with guilt, and it was holding him back from seeing her. It all made sense now, and he hated himself.

Conrad's determination to go to the funeral prompted him to have another drink, and he rationalized he needed a crutch considering the situation, the same alcoholic crutch he had utilized so many times in the past. When he was ready to leave after downing several drinks, he took the crutch with him, a small bottle of vodka. "Just in case," he told himself.

By the time he reached the Cedar Hills Cemetery the alcohol was boiling in his veins, and he was beyond being legally drunk. For some miraculous reason he was able to drive without incident, except for a couple of instances when the car drifted slightly out of its lane.

Conrad had parked with the other cars that he believed were gathered for Erica's funeral, and from what he could determine, was already in progress. Before he left the car, he took a couple of swigs of vodka for reinforcement, trying to enhance his confidence while he walked toward the crowd of people that had gathered a short distance away. Being intoxicated made him more aggressive than he had been feeling, but it also made him stumble and grab onto a tree to steady himself provoking him to say, "Ah shit, I'm freaking drunk, God damn it." Then he laughed out loud.

When Conrad was within fifty feet of the gravesite, he stopped. He strained his eyes which were tearing from the alcohol and the cool morning air so he could focus on the faces of the people that were grouped together. He noticed two women dressed in black. The taller one was the younger of the two, in her early twenties he guessed, with shoulder length blonde hair. She was extremely attractive, but her face manifested sadness. Conrad surmised it was Debbie, Erica's younger sister, and the other woman most likely was her mother. A tall, handsome gentleman was standing next to her, and he assumed he was Erica's father.

With cynicism Conrad thought, what a place and time to finally meet them, and they don't have a clue as to who the hell I am.

Conrad could hear the priest saying, "We all look upon death with great sadness when one of our beloved is taken. It is difficult for us to understand why our Father in heaven calls our loved one when He does. Yet, it is not for us to question His actions and infinite wisdom."

"Bullshit," Conrad blurted, interrupting the priest. "I know why He takes us and causes grief," and he moved closer, staggering as he stepped, drawing the attention of the mourners. "He hates all of us. Why else would He take such a beautiful girl so early in her life," Conrad continued with his verbal attack on God.

"Who is he?" one of the male bystanders asked of Conrad.

"Who am I?" Conrad snapped. "I'm a dear friend of Erica," and he started to weep.

"He's inebriated. Get him out of here," a Hollis family member commanded, and two funeral directors took hold of him to usher him away.

"Wait," Debbie called out. "Leave him, alone," and she walked over to Conrad, the surprised members of the group focused on her with their eyes. She studied him for a moment, thinking she had recognized his voice from the phone call he had made on Saturday morning. "Are you by any chance Conrad?" Debbie asked.

"Yes, I am," and his voice conveyed sorrow.

"Conrad, I'm Debbie Hollis, Erica's sister. She talked about you often. I'm sorry we had to meet this way. You're welcome to join us."

He was momentarily taken by her kindness and compassion, but he knew he was wasted. "I'm sorry for my conduct," he slurred. "I'll be all right here. I didn't mean any harm," he tried to apologize, and he stared at her with his eyes asking forgiveness.

He had used the word harm, the same word used by the physic in his dream. The Hollis family knew nothing about it, and it was so ironical. To him it was a word of infamy, and he would remember its terrible meaning for the rest of his life.

"Thanks for coming," Debbie said, and she hugged him for one moment and shared his grief for the loss of Erica.

Conrad walked away, occasionally staggering, and as he did he heard the priest continue with the service. When he reached his car, his mood was sullen with the realization he would never see Erica again.

He seated himself in the car, and then looked back at the gravesite. It made him weep, and occasionally he wiped the tears from his face. Then he picked up his cell phone and called Charlene.

"This is Charlene," and he was relieved to hear her voice.

"Charlene, this is Conrad. I'm wasted, and I need you," and she knew something was terribly wrong by the sound of his voice.

"What's wrong?" she asked her voice anxious.

"I'm… I'm at the Cedar Hill Cemetery. A dear friend is being buried. Help me, Charlene," and she could detect the desperation in his plea.

She didn't need any details now. All she knew was that he needed her and that he was terribly upset and wasted.

"I'll find you. Please stay put, and I'm on my way."

She was leaving now. He could always depend on her. She had always been there for him before, and he knew she wouldn't let him down now. She was such a good friend. Yes, such a good, dependable friend, and as he thought about it his head fell back against the headrest.

Conrad had no idea how long it took Charlene to find him. All he knew was that she was there in the car comforting him.

"Don't leave me, Charlene. Don't ever stop being my good friend," he was pleading.

"I won't, I won't," she kept insisting. "You know I'd do anything for you, anything," she assured him. "I'll never leave you alone again. I want to take care of you for as long as you want me to."

"Good," he slurred, and he patted her arm with his hand. He leaned over and rested his head against her bosom, and as she held him her contact made him feel a sense of security. "Take me home, Charlene. Please take me home now," he said as he started to drift from consciousness. A moment later his eyes were closed.

CHAPTER 29

The late morning air was crisp, and patches of fluffy, white cumulus clouds dotted the sky, casting large, spotty shadows on the ground. Conrad was seated on a white, wrought iron chair across from a matching table that held a newspaper, a bottle of vodka, a pitcher of orange juice, and a glass holding the contents of a recently made drink.

He was at his parents home by circumstance and not choice. The condo had started to close in on him and he needed to get away. He had decided to take a week off from work to give him time to pull himself together. Charlene had pleaded vehemently to stay with him so that she could tend to his needs, but he had insisted that she return to work.

He hadn't read a single word of the newspaper. Instead, his mind was immersed in the recollection of events that had transpired over the past several days. Life had been a bitter experience. If life could have been transformed into a human being, he would have pounded relentlessly on its face until he had battered it senseless. Only then could he have achieved some vindication releasing the aggressions that he had built up inside.

Conrad sat, continuing to exhaust his mind with thoughts about the harsh realities of the past, and thoughts about his future. There was Charlene who could be classified as a staunch ally and friend. Of course, there was always the possibility they could become lovers. Then there was Debbie Hollis. Superficially, she was a living doll, and he wondered if she was anything like Erica. Being Erica's sister, he already felt a bond to her. Perhaps he could call on her and make her acquaintance, perhaps.

Conrad rose from the chair and walked to the other side of the gazebo. He inhaled deeply the crisp air several times, feeling revitalized with each deep breath. He closed his eyes momentarily, listening to the melodic sounds and songs of the wild birds that detached him from his troubled existence. But his detachment was short lived when he saw his mother approaching the gazebo.

The first emotion he felt was resentment, expecting her to expound on his ethics of work and responsibility. "What brings you out this lovely morning to join me, mother?" he said reaching for his drink.

"To join you in a short conversation," and Constance seated herself at the table.

A short conversation, he thought. That was a pleasant surprise. But what was her definition of short? He really was in no mood to listen to any of her commentary that usually centered on criticism.

"I'm sorry to hear about your friend Erica," she said with sincerity. "I didn't realize the depth of your relationship with her. I understand she was a lovely girl. We should talk more often, Conrad. Your life is somewhat clandestine from your father and me. We really care what happens to you whether or not you believe it," and she studied him for a moment. "If you ever feel a need to talk, I'll be more than happy to listen," and she rose from the chair. "See, I told you it was going to be a short conversation. Take care, Conrad," and she headed back to the house.

He was shocked. His mother had manifested a sense of compassion, which must have journeyed into her heart from some unknown source. He had never noticed either of his parents being emotional, affectionate beings. And he never saw them display any such emotion, at least not to him, and he had no real recollection of being cuddled and kissed. It made him wonder how he became such an emotional being. Obviously, it had to be in some family genetics of past generations that sadly did not include his parents. Only one emotional being could understand another.

Conrad sat back in the chair and closed his eyes. Again he started to think. Abigail had scared his heart permanently. In the process of getting even, he had caused his friend Ed great pain and had destroyed their friendship. Penny Hennessey was a victim of deceit and had committed suicide. And Erica tragically lost her life, and no matter how he tried to reason, he was indirectly responsible.

Fate and life had conspired against him. But why, what had he done which was so terrible that he deserved to be confronted with such a conspiracy in the first twenty-six years of his life?

He finally concluded life was reminiscent of a pugilist in the ring. And every human being was a pugilist. There were several rounds to be fought in life and its challenges. He himself already had fought several tough, bitter rounds and had been knocked off his feet. He had been hurt badly, but he wasn't out, and he was going to keep fighting. Yes, there was still plenty of fight left in him.

He raised his glass of vodka and orange juice and said, "To life the predator, and relentless pugilist." He laughed cynically before he drank the glass dry. Then he made himself another drink.

CHAPTER 30

Three months later

"Doctor Kurri will see you now Mr. Hill," the receptionist was saying, and she led him to the psychiatrist's office. Conrad knew the routine well, for he had had six previous sessions, and hopefully, this would be his final session.

"How do you feel this afternoon Conrad?" Dr. Kurri addressed him after he was seated.

"I feel good, Doctor," he answered in earnest. "As a matter of fact, I really feel I have found closure and no longer have a need for any additional sessions."

Dr. Kurri studied him for a moment and then said, "That's good to hear, Conrad. Such an attitude puts you on the road to recovery. Let's talk about it. Can you tell me why you think you are ready for closure?" she asked.

Conrad re-positioned himself in the chair to get more comfortable before he spoke. "I don't feel the same way I did when Abigail left me. The intensity of the initial hurt has abated."

"And exactly what feeling was that?" Dr. Kurri asked.

"I no longer feel the hatred and animosity, or the urge to get even. I guess I was really overwhelmed when it all started, and I really lost it," and Dr. Kurri could see he was remorseful. "All I wanted was for them to feel the pain that I had felt," he informed her.

"It's not unusual to feel what you did, Conrad. You experienced trauma, and we all have a threshold of what we can handle. We all react differently to certain stimuli."

Dr. Kurri flipped open a small note pad on her desk and leaned back in her high backed chair before she continued speaking, occasionally glancing at the note pad.

"You had a serious problem, Conrad. But you recognized it and didn't like the person you had become. The consequences of your behavior made you seek help, and I believe the sessions you have had have brought you to where you currently are, to the person you once knew and liked," and she smiled approvingly. "I also feel you are ready for closure."

"Thank you, Dr. Kurri. I couldn't have done it without you," and he was truly grateful.

Dr. Kurri walked out to Conrad and shook his hand. "You know where to find me if you should ever need help, Conrad. Remember, we all need help now and then. The best advice I can give to patients is to always be honest, and the real key is to recognize there is a problem and try to resolve it. If the problem requires professional help, then get it," and she couldn't stress it enough.

"Thank you again, Dr. Kurri," a grateful Conrad iterated.

When Conrad left the building, he felt good and relieved. He felt a portion of his life, a part he truly regretted had been removed from his existence, and a part he never wanted to relive. He was ready to move on with his life, and with the assurance of Dr. Kurri, he was convinced it was the right time and thing to do.

Two weeks after his last session with Dr. Kurri, Conrad decided he would get in touch with Debbie Hollis. It was early afternoon when he reached her by phone. "Debbie, this is Conrad Hill."

"What a surprise, Conrad. It's nice to hear from you."

"Thank you, Debbie. How are you doing?" and he sincerely hoped she was coping well with the death of her sister.

"As well as you can expect, I guess. I miss Erica very much," and it was more than Debbie had imagined what the adjustment would be like.

He hesitated for a moment and then said, "I do too." Conrad moistened his lips before he spoke. "Debbie, I was wondering if you were free and if I could meet you at Massey Park around three this afternoon? I'd like to talk to you, and it's Okay if you can't make it. I realize this is short notice."

"Well, it so happens I'm not busy this afternoon. I'd be happy to meet you. Where will I find you?"

He was pleased she could meet him. She had been on his mind a great deal, and he wasn't really sure why. "Why don't you meet me by the pond benches in the area where the people feed the ducks," said Conrad.

"Sure, and I'll see you at three this afternoon," and she wondered what his motive was for the meeting.

When Debbie met Conrad at the park, she gave him a warm hug.

"It's nice to see you, Debbie," and he smiled warmly. "Would you like to walk a little?" he asked.

"Sure, it's a nice day to walk."

"You are probably wondering what I have to say, Debbie. I really know nothing about you except for the little tidbits of information offered by your sister."

"I hope she said good things about me. Isn't that what I'm supposed to say?" and she smiled at him.

"Rest assured, I only heard good things," and he was silent for a moment. Then he said, "You are probably wondering why I wanted to talk to you," he repeated.

"Frankly, I am curious," she answered.

"Speaking honestly, Debbie, I was very fond of your sister, and I was falling in love with her."

"From what Erica told me about your relationship, Conrad, I'm not surprised."

As they approached a park bench Conrad said, "Would you like to sit down for a spell?"

"That sounds fine," she accepted, still wondering if Conrad had something personal to discuss with her.

A moment later, Conrad spoke. "I hope I'm not coming on too strongly, but I want to be truthful with you, Debbie. I want you to know I feel a strong bond to you, and yes, it does have something to do with Erica. After all, she was your sister," and he felt relieved finally saying it.

Debbie studied Conrad for a moment. "I can understand that, Conrad. And I honestly feel something for you even though I hardly know you," and she smiled warmly at him. "There is no question Erica is a common bond between us," she continued.

Her words were so comforting to him, and she had no idea how much. He liked her the first time he had encountered her at Erica's funeral. He was drunk at the time, but he recalled how compassionate she had treated him in his moment of grief. She had asked him to stay even though two men attending the funeral were ready to force him to leave the grave site.

Conrad found the conversation going in the direction he was hoping for, namely Debbie being receptive to him. He would continue with his selective dialogue.

"If it's okay with you, Debbie, I'd like the chance to get to know you better, and that would include dating. I hope you don't construe this to mean I want to date you on the rebound. I just want to take it on a day to day basis if it's okay with you so I can get to know Debbie Hollis, the person," and his eyes embraced her.

"I'm flattered, Conrad, I really am," and she brushed her hair back with her hand. Before she spoke, she hesitated a moment as if to process what he just said. "I'd like that, Conrad."

"That's great," and he was visibly pleased.

Conrad turned his body to face Debbie and raised his arm with his palm up and said, "Here's to getting acquainted," and Debbie slapped his palm with the palm of her hand.

They both laughed and Debbie repeated the words, "To getting acquainted."

"I'm glad I talked to you today. Thank you for meeting me," and he was grateful.

"The pleasure is mine, Conrad, and I'm pleased you called."

When Conrad returned to his condo, the first thing he did was mix a drink. Then he seated himself in his favorite armchair by the fireplace where he so often collected his thoughts. He lifted the drink he prepared—which was seated on the end table by his chair—and drank from it. After he put it down, his thoughts immediately shifted to Debbie Hollis.

While he had conversed with her earlier in the day, he had observed so many good qualities about her. It was apparent she possessed a certain presence that was both angelic and tranquil. She was soft spoken and amiable, and he felt extremely comfortable in her company. Her smile was warm with a sensual under-lip, and he marveled at the clean purity of her profile. Her flaxen colored hair was at shoulder length and caressed her face. And how could he forget her vivid, gentian blue eyes that were alert and attentive, and graced with long, elegant eyelashes. She definitely was a charming, beautiful, young woman, and Conrad was exuberant with the thought of dating her.

Some months ago he had crossed over to the other side of love when his body was consumed with hatred and revenge. Now there was nothing more important than to pursue and experience a new existence. Perhaps he would find it with Debbie Hollis, perhaps. But one thing was certain. He needed and was ready to love again.